Molding Lives

Molding Lives

MOLDEANDO VIDAS
(English Version)

PRISCILA GOTAY

Molding Lives

Copyright © 2019 by Priscila Gotay. All rights reserved.

No part of this publication may be reproduced, stored in a retrieval system or transmitted in any way by any means, electronic, mechanical, photocopy, recording or otherwise without the prior permission of the author except as provided by USA copyright law.

The opinions expressed by the author are not necessarily those of URLink Print and Media.

1603 Capitol Ave., Suite 310 Cheyenne, Wyoming USA 82001
1-888-980-6523 | admin@urlinkpublishing.com

URLink Print and Media is committed to excellence in the publishing industry.

Book design copyright © 2019 by URLink Print and Media. All rights reserved.

Published in the United States of America

ISBN 978-1-64367-465-0 (Paperback)
ISBN 978-1-64367-464-3 (Digital)

15.05.19

Contents

Introduction 7

I:	Conscience Awakening	9
II:	Taking the Mask Off a Monster	17
III:	A Crucial Age	31
IV:	A New Challenge, Let's Face It	43
V:	The Challenge Is Still On; Be On the Alert	48
VI:	Words Shape Up Realities	61
VII:	The Reward For Being Firm and Constant	68
VIII:	Practical Recomendatios	72

Conclusion 83
Epilogue 85

Introduction

As I observe how difficult has been for many parents and care givers to deal with the great responsibility and mission of instilling in children the set of values and principles, that would mold their character to be prepared to face the future, I was inspired to write this book.

It's worrisome to see so many kids getting out of control, even at an early age. As a mother of four children, that throughout the years have proven that the strategies I used while raising them worked, I feel that I should put a little stone on such an important project: the project of molding lives. If kids start to develop a good character from an early age, this would become a starting point of a line of benefits. For example: matured kids would become matured parents, whom at the same time would bring up their kids to become matured parents themselves, and so on.

My children are a good example of this; they have used my techniques with their children and have received very good results. If these strategies have worked for us, wouldn't they be an asset to those trying to succeed in such a project? Yet, it's very important to make sure your child's behavior is not a matter of a psychological or neurological condition.

The title MOLDING LIVES may take you to wonder: "Where am I going to find the correct mold for such a job?" Well, this is exactly the reason I am writing this book. My intention is to show the reader some ideas I used in the process of dealing with my children's behavior, as well as with my students, since I had the privilege to be a teacher who decided to work with children of all ages. I taught first to twelve grades for thirty-three years. This gave me the opportunity to observe and analyze the situations I encountered in dealing with children of different ages and backgrounds.

We all know that not every child is the same, therefore it is important to observe them individually, and make an analysis of their behavior in order to use the correct method for each one of them. And don't forget that it takes time and patience; but overall, love and understanding. Let's accept the challenge.

Chapter 1
Conscience Awakening

Train up a child in the way he should go, and when he is old, he will not depart from it.

Proverb 22:6

As you read this text, you may think it's a matter of religion. Most people feel that the word Bible means religion; but my intentions have nothing to do with a specific religion, or a way of thinking, but to awaken the reader's conscience that the truth implied in this message, and other Bible messages I will present later, could assist him or her in the process of guiding children to develop moral and spiritual values necessary to become citizens with the capacity to deal with life issues in a proper way, showing respect to their parents, siblings, teachers, neighbors, the officers of public order, etc.

We know that when we buy an electric appliance or other things, they come with a pamphlet with instructions on how to deal with them; but children do not. However, as I said before, there are many biblical principles that could guide us in such an important mission.

But there is something putting a stop to this, which is the law that provides freedom of religion. I have nothing against this law; I think it is good to allow people to worship or preach whatever their beliefs are. Yet, when the word Bible is mentioned, people may feel it is a matter of a specific religion. In the past, the Ten Commandments were explicit in public places; but due to that law, they were taken away, probably to prevent conflicts.

And my question is: "Shouldn't those principles be part of the education of the human being no matter what his or her belief is?" I personally think that everyone could reap good outcomes by keeping them, because they contain good advice on how to deal with every aspect of life.

As I already said, children do not bring a pamphlet of instructions on how to deal with them, but there is a book that contains biblical principles that, if put into practice, would help us raise our children with virtues such as honesty, responsibility, respect, and so forth; and it's the book of Proverbs of Solomon. These proverbs are a fountain of instructions for the development of our character from birth to old age. These proverbs are instructions for parents, as well as for their children.

One of those proverbs is the following: "Correct thy son and he shall give thee rest; yea, he shall give delight unto your soul" (Proverb 22:17) What a marvelous message! There is no greater satisfaction than to have well behaved children; but for that to happen it would be a good idea to follow Solomon's advice.

However, it is important to be aware that some of his proverbs suggest corporal punishment, which may create conflict with the Law of Child Abuse. This law was passed to protect children from being mistreated by parents or caregivers; but it's sad to say that, in a way, it has been counterproductive, because many kids are using it to intimidate their parents, mainly if they are not legal residents of our country, and I'm a real witness of this. While teaching in a town in the state of Florida, several mothers approached me with a great preoccupation because their children were misbehaving, and they were afraid of correcting them because they had the nerves to intimidate them with the law.

Let me present you an incident I witnessed during a teacher-parents meeting. My position at the school was ESOL teacher, which means English to Speakers of Other Languages, and periodically we had meetings with parents to discuss students' situations or any other matter. And something funny really happened. As the principal was presenting the issues related to the students, a Haitian lady stood up and asked for the opportunity to express herself.

She opened her conversation with the following question: "How many of you have ever had any problem with my kids?" No one raised the hand. She had three children at that school, one in the 10th grade, another in 11th, and the oldest in 12th grade. I was the English teacher of them all. No teacher had any complaint. And you want to know her reaction? In broken English she expressed the following message:

"You know why my kids are so good? Because I correct them. And even if I have to give them a good whipping, I do it. I'm not afraid of being deported, because they are my children, and it is my responsibility to raise them the correct way." I really admired the way she expressed herself because I believe it is crucial to let children know that we, parents, want our kids to be matured adults, ready to face life issues with wisdom.

There are times we have no other choice, but to give them a little spanking. If we have used all means to get their attention, with no result, we have to let them know we are in control. I should confess that I used the spanking and it really worked. And my kids appreciate it. As they grew older, they thanked me for doing that because they learned how to behave, not only at the house, but everywhere. To me it was better for them to suffer a little punishment at an early age, than to see them suffering by those situations they would encounter in life for not having clear in mind the moral and spiritual values so important in the process of becoming good citizens.

Solomon says it this way: "Chasten thy son while there is hope, …" (Proverb 19:18) To train a child while there is hope means to do it at an early age, because the time will come when it would be very hard to do it. But it is important not to go to the extremes. We should find constructive alternatives according to what's established. One of the alternatives I suggest is to take away any thing that they really enjoy; but he or she must know exactly the reason for the action.

Something else that could be a good trick is to pretend we are mad. One of my sisters used this trick and really helped her in dealing with her son. But for this to happen, there should be a good relationship between the child and the parent. When my nephew did something that my sister disapproved, she pretended to be mad at him. When he talked to her, she would not hold a conversation with him, but only a yes or a no, depending on what the situation was. This preoccupied him to the point that he would come to her and ask her to forgive him. He did not want his Mom to feel that way about him. By the way, he became a wonderful man all together.

My experience has been that a little whipping at an early age saved me and my children from having to encounter sad situations. If I would have ignored those early years to establish the set of rules and regulations based on some principles and moral values, things would have been different. However, don't think I punished them for any simple reason; I did it when they, in some way, showed lack of respect to me, their siblings or any other person. Lack of respect was not tolerated in our home.

It is important to know that if we have established a good relationship with our kids, they would never feel that we have mistreated them. The following is an example of what I am saying: One of my grandsons that was ten years old at the time, did something my daughter disapproved, and whipped him in a way I thought it was too harsh. But he surprised me with the following comment: "Grandma, don't forget that she didn't abuse me; she did it because I disobeyed her."

Why do you think he expressed himself this may? He did it because they had a good relationship as mother and son. He knew she loved him so much, that otherwise, she would have never punished him that way.

If we constantly use words that lower our children's self-esteem, and whip them for any silly reason, and besides this, do not show them love and affection, they will feel mistreated and will respond the same way. This is the reason we must add love and understanding to the process of correction.

Solomon's advice which I presented were directed to parents and or caregivers; but he also offers good advice to children, so they would be able to escape from different things that could affect their well-being, such as corruption, iniquity, wickedness and so on. If we as parents get in the habit of reading a proverb starting the first day of the month, at the end of it, we have gone through the whole book of proverbs. But it is important to give follow up, so the information would be fixed in their mind; and once it is there, it would become their way of living.

The principles implied in these proverbs could be a good method for the development of our character, regardless of what religious background or beliefs we have. My experience has been that by applying these Bible principles into practice while raising my children, have produced positive outcomes.

Besides Solomon's proverbs, the Apostle Paul's letters also give orientation to parents, as well as to their offspring, on how to handle the family relationship. The following message refers to the children. It says: *"Children, you must obey your parents in the Lord; for this is right. Honor your father and your mother (which is the first commandment with promise.) That it may be well with you, and you may live long on the earth."* (Ephesians 6:1- 3)

Many Christian parents constantly express this text to their children, but this is not the end of the message; it also talks to parents as follows: *"And you, parents, provoke not your children to wrath, but bring them up in the nurture and admonition of the Lord."* And in Colossians 3:21 Paul says it this way: *"Parents, provoke not your children to anger, so they won't be discouraged."* Saying this in today's vocabulary should read: So, they won't develop a low self-esteem.

It is sad to say, but many parents concentrate themselves on the first part of the text that is related to the children, and ignore the second part, which is so important in the process of raising children. And how does this happen? By ignoring their good actions and concentrating on their shortcomings; or by neglecting their need of affection. No matter how many good deeds a child does, to many adults is irrelevant; but if the child does the wrong action, the whole world would know.

Parents definitely, should apply this advice to the method of rearing their children because this way they won't be provoked to anger. In my opinion, many young guys get stranded, trying to find a way out of so many situations they encountered on daily basis. Many times, we as parents, on an effort to control our children, and with all our good intentions, make mistakes that force them to become rebellious.

Some kids are so intelligent, that their conduct, or the way they express themselves, may be confused with the idea that they are too nosy, disrespectful, or mean. And we, parents, on an effort to make them behave the way people feel they should, make the awful mistake of forcing them to be who they are not.

I should confess that I made this mistake with my first child, who was too bright for her age, and I did not have the knowledge of how to deal with the situation, which really affected her in a negative way. I'm not saying that she is not a good person; what I am trying to say is that, if I would have had some information on how to deal with a smart child, she would have been a happier one.

But as I considered the outcomes of demanding certain way of behavior instead of guiding the child through the process, helped me in the process of educating my youngest son who happened to be very bright for his age, and outspoken. This time I was able to manage him in a way that really satisfied both of us. I followed the apostle's advice of not provoking our children to anger, so their self-esteem would not be affected in a negative way. Yet, I was very firm and constant with him.

Do not think I was too lenient; he, sometimes had a little whipping; but I took my time to talk to him, always letting him know the reason for the discipline, adding to it love, affection and understanding.

If we understand the meaning of the verb to train, which is the main subject of this book, we would realize that many times we do not train the child, but just demand good behavior, or just ignore bad behavior, and both extremes are wrong. In my opinion, this has been one of the reasons so many young guys are so disgusted. They resent the way they were treated from their childhood, which prevented them from developing their self-control which is so important to deal with life issues.

The verb to train means to discipline, mold, guide, encourage and nurture. In other words, to give specific instructions and skills, or specific orders, in a systematic method. This implies that

we should create some specific and systematic patterns of conduct, and a series of rewards and sanctions, to enforce the conduct expected. This is the message implied in the title of this book. But what should be the correct age to start this mission? From birth.

As a mother and a retired teacher, who had gone through many experiences, I consider myself capable of putting a little stone on such an important project, (as I already expressed), the project of molding lives. I do not want the reader to think I was the perfect mother or teacher, since I also made mistakes, but as I was maturing, I developed some strategies, that really helped me in the project of helping kids to develop good character, so they would become people with honesty, responsibility, and submitted to the rules and regulations established, which are crucial for a successful life.

I am presenting some strategies, and anecdotes that may sound funny, or out of the norm, which I consider to be helpful for anyone interested in making a difference while dealing with children and young adults.

The title MOLDING LIVES may sound a little odd, since molding comes from the noun mold.

If you are baking a cake, you need a mold that will give you the exact characteristics of the cake you are going to bake. But now you may ask yourself: "Where am I going to find a mold to shape up my children's life?" This is exactly the challenge. We know that each child is a different person; therefore, we must observe their character to develop the correct mold, suitable to each one of them.

It is well known that in the past there were methods to correct children that were too drastic. One of them was to kneel the child down on a rough surface such as a metal grater or sand.

My mother sometimes asked me to kneel down to pray as a strategy to correct me, which took me to think praying was punishment.

But although my mom sometimes was so tough when correcting me, she also took time to instill in me the moral and spiritual values that made me the person I am. This also helped me in the process of raising my children because I used what I considered positive from her way of dealing with my education, disregarded what I thought was too drastic, and added some of the advice I learned from the Bible.

I mixed all this with some of the modern disciplinary techniques which I considered favorable for the project of dealing with children and young adults, which resulted on the development of this work, which I consider a good resource in the mission of developing good citizens.

The main reason for taking my time to write this book has to do with my interest in helping people know they are not alone in the mission of dealing with children. The strategies I present may be a good resource to assist the ones in charge of such an important task. I want the reader to know that most of the ideas presented in this book are based on the conclusions I reached as a mother and as a teacher, and that this did not happened over night, as I emphasize; it was a process.

My genuine preoccupation is the education and character development of the future generation. Today's children are the ones who would have the future of the world in their hands. If their education is not founded on the moral values necessary for the development of a good character, how would the future generations be? Our duty should be to help children develop a scale of values which are necessary for the development of a high self-esteem. But for this to happen, they need to know who they are, and be aware of what is right and what is wrong. But understand that the results would not come over night. It takes patience and understanding, but also firmness, and affection.

In conclusion, I want to repeat that the ideas presented in this book are based on the conclusions I reached while dealing with children. It is my greatest desire that this information, would be of great help in the process of developing the character of children, who are precious jewels in our hands. Let's take good care of them!

Chapter II
Taking the Mask Off a Monster

As you read this title you probably wonder what would be in my mind to express myself this way. According to my observation, I think there are some issues preventing us from managing children's education the proper way. If we auto-exam ourselves while reading this chapter, we may find some points we have overlooked; not because we are bad parents, but for lock of knowledge. This is the reason I present this information before getting to the main subject of the book which is MOLDING LIVES.

However, as I already mentioned, I want to let the reader know that the information presented are based on the personal observations, evaluation and conclusions I have reached throughout my life as a mother and a teacher, plus what I see around in the communities where I have lived, that led me to discover many issues that are affecting, in a negative way, our good intentions; issues which I compared to a monster that we have to face on daily basis.

And what arms do we need to confront and overcome such a monster? Well, by reading and evaluating all those points I am presenting, if the reader feels that there is something he or she needs to change or improved, work on it.

> *To begin, let me put as first point that for kids to develop good qualities, they need to have good models.*

And the question is: How can this be possible if, since kids are born, they are exposed to different models? It is obvious that on daily basis, families encounter financial problems that force both parents to work outside of their homes, delegating their kids' care to other people, many times to strangers, that may have different sets of values. What is permissible for someone, may not be for another, or the other way around. This could even affect their self-esteem. They may not realize who they should follow.

In the past, this was not something common because there was the extended family, that provided a sense of security to them, because they felt they belonged to a family. If the mother was not there, there was the grandma, or an aunt. They also had cousins and neighbors as playmates. But now a days it is not the same.

The opportunity that families have to move to different places is an effort to live a better life, have put a distance among the family members, which I consider to be one of the reasons for the situation we are facing. Since they do not have a specific model to follow, many children and young adults have not been able to develop a good personality.

Another thing I personally think has affected the development of children's personality is the centralization of the elementary schools. To me, those early grades are very important for such a mission. In the past, the elementary schools were part of each neighborhood. This was very favorable because parents and teachers had a closer relationship. The students were aware that if they got into trouble, their parents would know it right away. And many parents drop by school every now and then, to see how their kids were doing.

Another thing I consider good for the children of that time was that their neighbors and cousins were classmates, which created in them emotional security. And something else I liked was that some of the neighbors helped each other with keeping an eye on the kids.

By presenting these issues I am not pretending to say that in the past everything was perfect; every now and then conflict may arise; but in comparison, now a days the situation has become unbearable. But going back is out of this world.

The instability our children are going through has created in many of them a sense of insecurity. Many of them do not know their real identity; this is the reason we should look for alternatives to deal with this issue. We need to be conscientious that our children need to feel that they have a family. Therefore, we need to adjust so there would be good communication among the family members in general.

It is sad to say, but many times parents worked extra hours, and even extra days for the family to enjoy material things, but nothing should substitute a good parent children's relationship. If both parents must work, then it is very important to find a little time to pay attention to their children's needs which include affection, love and understanding. They need to be heard and guided on the right path.

> ***The second point to emphasize is the following: Parents need to be on the same page when establishing the rules and regulations their children need to follow for the well-being of the family in general terms.***

This is the ideal thing to do; but sometimes it doesn't happen. Parents must agree on what is expected of their children, the rewards for good behavior, and the sanctions for not doing the right thing. If they enforce the values in a constant manner, this would create in them a sense of responsibility that would not let them go stranded.

If we follow apostle Paul's advice, there would be a better understanding among the members of the families. **He asks wives to summit to their husbands, but also asks husbands to love their wives as they love their own bodies.** (Ephesians 5 verses 21, 22, 25 and 28) **Then he continues with an advice to children. He asks them to obey and honor their parents that it may be well with them.** (Ephesians 6: verses 1, 2 and 4)

This issue may be controversial to some people because they may confuse the idea of being firm and constant, with provoking them to wrath; so we need to know the difference. When we correct a child by being firm and constant; but using words that would lead them to understand the good intention of the message we are trying to transmit to them, they would be more eager to accept it; although at that instant, they may show disagreement.

I experienced this with my kids. When we had disagreement with something they wanted to do, they went to their rooms showing some disgust for a little while, but later they would come to me and offered an apology. This took me to think that when they went to their rooms, they thought about the intention behind my message, and realized I was right.

But on the other hand, if we use words that lower their self-esteem, and beat them up for any silly thing without giving them the opportunity to explain what happened, this would provoke them to anger. It is good to give them a second chance by being aware that changes do not happen overnight. If we are unaware of this, we are providing the reasons for them to become rebellious because they feel they have been disrespected.

If we made an analysis of all those points Paul presents for us to enjoy a good family relationship, we may realize that the base for so many personality problems has to do with the lack of submission. If children see a good relationship between their parents, there is a greater possibility that they would submit to them, and this would provide for a better relationship among all the family members; otherwise, it could become a vicious cycle, since a bad attitude would provoke someone else to react the same way, and this could go on, and on, to the point it may seemed that an agreement would never be reached. Let's not overlook Paul's advice for submission.

> ***As third point, there is something, I consider to be provoking a vicious cycle. It's sad to say, but there are parents that were victims of child abuse; and as parents, they treat their children the way they were treated; or they may do the opposite of this by becoming too lenient.***

This is really a sad reality. It is well known that there have been many cases of children mistreated by their own parents, trying to follow what their parents did to them. Probably you feel I am talking about corporal punishment only; but there is the psychological mistreatment which is even worst than the other. If the child feels lonely, misunderstood, disrespected, neglected, ridiculed, put down, compare to other kids, and so forth, their esteem becomes low. Then they may tend to find relieve by taking the wrong path, offered by some other kids that may be dealing with the same situation.

Yet, there is the other side of the same issue, which is the following: Some parents, in an effort to avoid their children to experience the situations they went thorough as children, may become too lenient, which may be counterproductive. These children, for not being guided in the process of developing the scale of values that will make of them people of honor; people with personal satisfaction that would show respect and responsibility, they will experience disappointment and frustration. We should auto-exam ourselves to see if, in one way or another, we are provoking our children to behave the way they are behaving.

> ***The fourth point to present has to do with those parents that want their kids to have those material things they longed for during their childhood.***

These parents, with their best intention, have sacrificed their children's education and discipline, so they can enjoy, what-ever material thing they would like to have, such as good clothes, bikes, electronics, and even a car, which may motivate them to become arrogant; and worse of all, since they have not learned the real value of things, when they are no longer depending on their parents, will suffer the consequences.

Even if we are in the position of providing those things, we should take our time to let them know that enjoying all those material things should not take the priority, but the development of the necessary skills that will enable them to earn a living in the future, adding to this the moral values that will lead them to become people with dignity; human beings capable of dealing with life issues in a mature way.

However, providing them things that are not a priority, may be used as an incentive to get their attention on the objective we have in mind. I think there are things they should get only if they deserve them. If they get what they want no matter how they are behaving, may be counterproductive.

> *Something that may be affecting, in a negative way, the important task of rearing our children with the values and education that will enable them to become good citizens is, that there are parents so interested on seeing their kids being outstanding in what they do, but they don't take their time to make sure that what they're doing is done with honesty.*

It is very important to follow up our children to see how they are getting their good grades. There are students who cheat on the tests because their parents are very demanding, and for them to be on the save side, they cheat. We need to check and see why they aren't succeeding, instead of forcing them to have good grades by means of threat.

Other kids may cheat while participating on sports, or competition, and their parents are so proud of their triumph, without the notion that they have been cheating. It is important to let our children know that not everyone will be the winner of a competition. If they are concerned about this, they will be able to be honest. However, we should encourage them to practice and to put all their effort on the competition, so they will be proud of themselves if they become winners. They should know that if they cheat, sooner or later, the truth will come up making them ashamed of their actions.

> *The following point may sound odd. There are parents who were very pampered by their parents, but when they became parents, because of certain situation they had suffered, they decided to neglect the affectionate stage of their kids.*

Everyone is born with the need of affection. This is a very important aspect of life we need to go thorough from birth. But sometimes it's neglected for different reasons. One of the reasons of this may have to do with the fact that some parents, when they were children, were pampered so much, but due to an unexpected life circumstance, they were taken away from this type of environment, and this made them suffer so badly, that when they become parents, they decide to avoid giving their children too much affection, to prevent them from going through the same painful experience they went though, if by any chance, something happens to them as parents.

This may be a reason so many of them end up on the arms of other beings that offer them a little love and affection, which may be the wrong companionship. Or they may not end up this way, but may become shy, with a low esteem; thinking that nobody loves them.

> *Other types of parents are those who trying to make good money to give their kids the best, spend so much time working extra hours, neglecting communication with their kids.*

Communication between parents and children should not be neglected by no means.

This has been one of the reasons so many kids have stranded away from the correct path. They need to be listened to. If we do not have the correct response for their preoccupation, let's look for information.

Remember that the time will come when the opportunity to talk to them would not be there. The material things would pass away, but a good relationship among the members of the family, should never stop.

This situation could affect children in different ways. The father of a friend of mine was so busy all the time, that neglected the communication with his two sons. One of them was a friendly guy who found comfort with good friends. He was a very good and hardworking student to the point of becoming a doctor in bilingual education. But his brother was so sad and disgusted with his father's lack of communication, that became depressed. He really was not motivated.

This situation moved him to confront his father and told him that he really did not care for so many material things he was providing him, that he really missed a good father and son relationship. And he closed the confrontation with the following words: "When I needed your support, you weren't there." Therefore, it is crucial to be aware of the needs of a child, which may not always be material things.

> ***There is another situation that's creating a crisis, which is that there are too many adolescents having kids.***

This issue may be a little controversial because there are exceptions to the rule. I, personally, know of two cases of teenage girls thirteen and fourteen, who became wonderful mothers. They raised good children and have been with same husband for many years. But they were fortunate to have married matured men, not teenagers. If teenagers start having children without being prepared to support the family, and to deal with all the needs of the family, what would be the outcome? Inexperienced parents would produce imbalanced children.

> ***What about those kids whose parents cast aside, never showing them that they are as important as their siblings? This could be a reason many children show bad behavior.***

It is sad to say, but there are parents who expect all their kids to act the same way. This idea takes them to express themselves as follows: "Why aren't you like your sister/brother?" But they may not know that everybody is different. In the family there may be a child who is very quiet and relaxed, but another, the other way around. There may be a child very serious with his school work, while another may take school lightly. In fact, there are different characters.

But the problem comes up when parents start to compare them showing more interest and paying more attention to whom they consider a better child. What parents should do is to evaluate the character of each one, by observing them in different situations; and this way they will discover that every child has virtues that need to be re-enforced by the way the adults in charge of them, praise him or her. But it is sad to say that many times parents miss the opportunity to enjoy their kids' virtues because they pay more attention to the shortcomings than to the good deeds.

My advice is not to compare your children with no other child. When a child feels inferior to a sibling, two things could happen: he/she may develop a low self-esteem considering him or herself inferior to anybody else. Or he/she becomes rebellious, disobedient, bully, etc. They tend to look for attention by showing bad conduct. Both outcomes are very bad.

Parents should demonstrate to their kids that every one of them has the same rights and privileges, so they could feel respected, loved and protected. They should notice that even though they are different beings, they have equal treatment. Otherwise, their self-esteem would be affected in a negative way.

> ***And the last point to discuss, which I consider is preventing many parents from taking control of their kids' behavior is THE LAW OF CHILD ABUSE.***

I have nothing against this law. I know it was necessary to pass this law to protect many children who were being mistreated, not only by their parents, but also by some care givers and even some teachers. The problem is that many kids are using the law to intimidate their parents when they are getting ready to correct them. This situation is forcing parents to neglect the enforcement of good behavior to avoid being reported by their children.

These parents are preoccupied for the way their kids are getting away from the set of values they have tried to instill in them. It is sad to say, but the law that is supposed to protect the children, in a way, has become counterproductive. I think that this law was not set up to prevent parents from correcting their children if they don't go to the extreme; but some kids are using it to intimidate their parents. And I'm aware of this because a few mothers approached me with such preoccupation.

Some people think child abuse is physical or corporal punishment only, but there's a form of abuse which affects the child's personality, and it's the psychological mistreatment. In my opinion, this is worse than the physical punishment. When this abuse takes place in the life of a child, *is* more painful than a belt whipping because he/she may develop a low self-esteem which is very difficult to deal with.

In my opinion, the worse punishment a child would receive is not being corrected at an early age. If we do not develop a good method of discipline to guide them on the correct path, they will become victims of the negative outcomes.

In the past, even the teachers would spank a child for misbehaving. Parents would whip their children, and even grandparents, and aunts and uncles. We knew we could not get away scot-free.

My mother told us that the teacher was our second mother, and it was okay for her to whip us if we misbehaved. But today is a different story. Many kids are disrespectful to parents, neighbors, teachers, members of the public order, etc.

This is the reason prisons are full of young fellows, that for not developing good character, have incurred in delinquent acts. And there are many others who are not in jail; but are prisoners of life itself which has been tough on them. Some are drug addicts trying daily, somehow, to find their supply. This is the reason I never allowed my kids to intimidate me with the law.

When my youngest was eight years old, incurred on a misconduct; and when I was getting ready to give him a little spanking, he said to me: "Hey, Mommy, don't you know there's a law that if parents punish their children could end up in jail?"

"Oh yes?" I said. "But let me tell you that if you disrespect me, I'd break your leg and then call the police and tell them to come for me because I've broken my son's leg, so you people won't bust his head in the future."

This was an exaggeration on my part. I was not going to break his leg at all. I just wanted to let him know that I was in control. And believe you me, I had to be firm and constant, and loving in the process of guiding him to become the person he is. As a little child he was outspoken and mean, but the way I dealt with his conduct produced a wonderful person.

After reading this information from the beginning of the chapter, I think you have noticed how a situation created another situation, which I call a chain reaction. It was obvious how a way of behavior provoked a negative reaction along the way. And how could we break this vicious cycle?

Observing the situation from the outside, is not the same as living the situation in person. I understand that if the family relationship has become a crisis, it may be difficult to deal with it, but not impossible. And do not forget that things may look impossible for us, but for God is possible.

When my kids were becoming teenagers, by observing how many youngsters (even some of the ones who were raised going to church) were becoming victims of drugs and other bad habits, I had no other choice, than to talk to God, who was the one who gave me the privilege of becoming a mother, and said: "Lord, you have seen how the young community is becoming prisoner of bad habits and negative situations; therefore I ask you that just as you did to king Solomon when he asked you for wisdom, so he would be able to deal with his people, I come before your presence asking you for wisdom to continue to raise my kids in a way that they won't be out there incurring in bad habits, but neither as pampered children without the skills and character to face life issues in a matured manner."

I know this prayer was answered, for the way I started to deal with them. I developed a set of tricks and strategies that allowed me to guide them in the process of developing the moral and spiritual values necessary to become good citizens.

Many parents have delegated the development of moral values to the school and/or the church; and haven't taken their time to do it themselves. I personally believe that this process should begin at home, as early as the child's birth, and re-enforced by the school and the church. This is really the thesis of this work. We must instill in our children the moral values and principles at an early age, so they would be able to manage life in a matured way. But don't forget that this process should be backed up by the way we, as matured adults, behave. What we do weighs more than what we say.

It is very important to talk to them about how rewarding life would be if they submit to some principles that would make them citizens of good character, which is shown by the way they behave. *If they follow these principles, they will become honest, responsible, truthful, friendly, considerate, and hardworking young guys; capable of dealing with life in a mature manner, which I am constantly repeating.* And we, as parents, will be relaxed knowing they are doing fine. There is nothing more rewarding for parents than to know their children are doing fine.

Although I don't consider myself an authority in psychology, neither in sociology, the strategies I used to deal with my kids and students' behavior, that really worked for me, I think may be helpful to parents and other people in charge of kids, who are worried about how the future generations would be.

But it is important to let you know that I made myself aware that my children's submission to the rules was not out of being scared, but out of love and the good intension of seeing them succeed in life by being good. I always explained to them the reason for my rules and regulations.

And I closed any issue I was dealing with, the following way: "Do you know why I'm doing this? I'm doing it because I love you so much, that I don't want to see you suffering on the hands of the authorities; neither on the hands of life itself, which many times brings hardships that require wisdom to deal with."

Although the theme of this book sounds like it was designed to help parents of very young children, (which I consider the right way to start the training, as Solomon's proverb presents) I also present strategies that I used to deal with teenagers, that really worked. Even if your child has reached adolescence showing a bad attitude, they could be restored. But it requires patience and understanding. Sometimes parents, out of ignorance, commit certain errors in dealing with their children. But it is helpful to examine the situation, and if there have been lock of consideration, or an injustice in dealing with the case, go to the child and ask for forgiveness.

This issue may sound out of proportion, but we should keep in mind that growing is painful, and many times in the process, kids are under a lot of stress. I practice this strategy, mostly with my youngest boy who was difficult to handle as a young child. If I considered I was too tough, I'd apologize to him. But if he really deserved the treatment, that was it. By doing this I gained his respect. He stayed in his room for a while, and later would come to me and said: "Mommy, could you forgive me?" And my answer was: "Of course I forgive you; but remember that I'm your mother who deserves respect and consideration." Then he would hug me.

As I present this information, it comes to me a mother/child conflict I observed at one of the schools I worked at. My teacher assistant had three daughters, but according to her, she was having conflict with the one in the middle, who at the time was fifteen years old. And one day, when we were having lunch at the school cafeteria, the girl showed up and told her something. Suddenly, the mother started to scold her in a way I considered out of proportion.

When the girl left, I approached my assistant with the following words: "Forgive me for being so frank with you, but I have to advice you that what you did to your daughter was not proper. You should have never scolded her in front of a stranger because this would make her even more rebellious."

Then I took advantage of this situation and brought up to her the times she had referred about her as very problematic, always contrasting her to the other two daughters. I also said that the reason this girl may be acting the way she did, was because she may be unhappy. This humble lady followed my advice, and started the project, which took her a while, and she succeeded.

A few years after I retired, I was at a shopping mall, and I happened to see this mother, who was there with a friend. We were so happy to see each other. And she surprised me with the following action. She introduced me to her friend as follows: "I want you to meet the person who gave me some strategies to deal with my daughter's behavior." Then she told me how wonderful her daughter had been doing.

I'm not presenting this information to brag about what a wonder woman I was. I just want to let my readers know that it's never too late to change attitudes, but that it requires observation, justice, encouragement, patience, and other virtues.

The information exposed in this chapter, which I entitled Taking the Mask Off a Monster, is to make people aware that there are many situations and expressions hindering the great challenge we encounter on daily basis. And how could we overcome it? By trying some of the tricks I used that really helped me with the great mission of MOLDING CHILDREN'S LIVES.

Chapter III
A Crucial Age

As I have already expressed, the process of training a child should begin from birth. If we observe some animals, we would see how they deal with their offspring. They always keep them near, feed them, protect them, and even play with them, but they also do something many human beings have neglected. They train them along the way, so they would be able to deal with their own environment. When they are ready, they are chased away to be on their own.

Yet, this is not happening with many of our children. That is why parents should be aware of the different stages a child goes through from birth to adulthood, to be able to deal with this matter, which I consider a project, using the correct tools. This way they would develop a good personality, which is something very important in the process of becoming successful when they become adults.

With this objective in mind, let me get to the main point which is the importance of guiding the child through the process of becoming matured beings. Every developmental stage a child goes through is important, but I consider the first stage as a crucial one. The term crucial means decisive or critical. This stage begins at birth and ends at age six. During this stage they become copy cats. They try to absorb what they see, hear or touch. Because at this time they have not developed the skills to analyze and evaluate what they see and experience, the adults should be alert, and ready to correct any wrong doing, and to re-enforce the good ones from the beginning.

We should take advantage of this early stage to do this, otherwise it would be a difficult task, because once some bad attitudes or habits are fixed in their personality, it would be a hard job to deal with them; although not impossible.

Now a day parents must establish patterns of conduct in a hurry, because kids enter school at an earlier age than in the past. Therefore, it's crucial to deal with this matter the sooner, the better, so they would be ready to handle the new environment. If they have developed a good scale of moral values, they would develop emotional stability, and firmness of character, that are qualities necessary for making the correct decisions.

Probably the reader would be wondering how could this be done at such an early age? Well, I'm not saying that it is going to be easy; but I would like to present some ideas I consider very useful in such a process.

To begin with, we must be aware that the first step we need to consider is the affectionate stage of the child, because it is very important for the development of their personality. We must pay attention to their physical needs in an orderly manner. It's very important to consider that the time and the way to feed the baby should be a priority, and it should follow a schedule.

Today, the idea of breastfeeding babies has been encouraged because is the natural way of feeding a child. For years this was something of the past, but scientific studies have proven the importance of it. Breastfeeding a child contributes to his or her physical, as well as emotional well- being. I'm so sorry for being one of the mothers who followed the new trend of my time, and used the artificial method, instead of the natural way. I remember when I used a pump to suck out my breast milk and poured it into the sink, instead of taking advantage of what nature had put in my hands. I was spending money, and time fixing the bottle to feed my babies. Isn't that something?

As I already said, breastfeeding a child contributes to his/her emotional well-being; but for many women this is not possible because they work outside. What could be an alternative to use?

Although nothing should substitute the natural way of feeding a baby, it's okay to use the artificial methods provided by the market. It's nothing wrong with it. But it's very important to hold the baby while bottle feeding him/her because this satisfies his/her need for affection. This action should be very satisfying to the baby as well as to the person feeding him/her. If the affectionate stage of the child is satisfied, it will produce in him/her a sense of security which is very important for the development of a positive self-esteem, which is necessary for the development of good character.

It's pitiful to say that the modern means available have made parents unconscious of children's affectionate need. It's easier to keep them in the playpen or on a stroller for long hours. And not only this, but provide them, even at a very early age, electronic devices such as tablets and cell phones to play on daily basis, not being aware of the damage they may provoke in the long run. Although these commodities, which I consider good if used with wisdom, make our life easier, they should never take the place of the personal affection between parents or care givers, and the child.

Another point I would like to present is how practical it is to deal with the child's needs before he or she starts screaming. As a personal experience, let me tell you that I was aware of my kids' needs before they started crying, which led some people wondered why it looked like there were no kids in my house. This was the result of not letting them be taken care of their needs when they started to scream. I didn't give them the chance to get what they wanted by crying.

I was aware that the strategy kids use to get what so ever they want is crying. If they realize that this strategy works, it becomes their powerful arm. However, don't think that they did not try this strategy when they were able to manipulate. Yes, sometimes they tried to get something by crying, but there I was prepared to handle the situation. I would tell them: "Wait a minute; don't come to me crying because I won't pay attention to you at all." They got away for a little while, but they came back later and expressed their desires in a normal way.

Yet, they also knew when the answer was no, because I always gave them the reason for it, which they accepted. We as parents should understand that although they feel disgusted at the time, the time will come for them to understand, that what we did, was with the intention to help them become mature citizens. This has been my personal experience.

From birth to preschool years, it is helpful to teach them the preschool skills just by talking to them in a normal way. This would help them with their cognitive development. Now a days many parents know this, but when I became a mother, I was criticized by some people because they thought doing this was out of the norm. But no matter their opinion, I continued to do this, and the result was very positive because my kids were able to talk at a very early age.

And you know how I taught them how to talk? When I was bathing them, I mentioned the body part I was washing; when I was dressing them, I mentioned the name and the color of the piece of clothes I put on them; while feeding them, I mentioned the name of the food, and also if it was hot or cold.

When they started to walk and I asked them to bring me something, I told them how many of what I wanted, the color and the position of the objects. This way they learned to talk at a very early age, something that surprised many people.

When my second child was two and a half years old, I went out with him and a lady saw him talking so clearly that she asked me why my son was not growing up. When I told her his age, she said: "Oh my God; I thought he was four." She thought he was four for the way he was expressing himself.

My children also had access to children books that had short illustrated writings that I used to encourage them to read. With them, they were able to learn the alphabet, the numbers, positions. And what was the outcome of all this? Well, this method made my life easier because when they started school, I did not have to deal with the task of re-enforcing those skills taught in school, because they had learned them at home as a natural way.

Now a days we are dealing with the reality that the cost of living has come up so high, that both parents have the need to go to work. In my opinion, even though this is a reality, parents should find a little time to be with their kids.

During this crucial stage, there is a special need kids have, that many times is not taken into consideration, which is the need to be respected. If children feel respected, they will show respect to others. This could be accomplished by letting them know that their belongings are respected. How would we feel if our things are taken away by another person just because he/she is older or younger? Throughout my life, I have noticed that the youngest child in a family has more privileges than their siblings.

I have observed in some households, that the youngest child has more privileges than the older siblings. If this child wants something that belongs to an older child, you could hear the parent saying: "Let him/her have it; he's/she's just a little kid." And sometimes they use words that lower the other child's esteem. How do you think this child would feel? His rights have been violated; this may produce in him/her, either a sense of rebellion or a low self-esteem.

And what about the youngest one? This one would feel superior than the others. He would feel he is in control, and this situation would provide the stage for conflicts among siblings, just because of the way parents, probably by ignorance, have violated their children's rights by taking sides.

Justice provides for the development of a healthy environment, in which love, respect and good disposition are promoted on daily basis, which is something very important for the emotional well-being of the family. If children's rights are violated, we cannot expect but conflict and bad behavior.

Kids should know from the beginning that the lack of respect won't be accepted. My kids knew this, and the strategies I used to encouraged them to respect each other. One thing I did was to make sure that their belongings were respected. They would ask permission if they wanted to take or play with something belonging to the other.

I would not allow any child to come home and try to take something from my kids, if they were not present. Apparently, I was mean by doing this, but I thought: "If I allow other kids to disrespect my kids' belongings, I am a hypocrite because I'm asking them to respect other people's belongings."

One of my many experiences I had which proofs that my method works is the following: When one of my sons was three years old, I went to visit a friend. When I got there, her son, who was just one year older, was playing with some toys. My son started to play with one of the boy's toys, and my friend said to me: "I think when you get ready to go, there will be a fight."

When I asked her why, she said: "Because your son has my son's toy and he may not want to let it go." Then, I asked her: "Do you think so? You'll see." As I was getting ready to leave, I said: "Abi, we need to go." The lady was shocked to see my son returning the toy, coming to my side and hold my hand to leave. He knew the toy wasn't his.

To develop in kids a sense of consideration for one another, would help them to become good citizens; but we, adults, should guide them, and over all, set a real example of what we are trying to teach; otherwise it would become a disaster.

Let's keep in mind that at birth what we bring is the instinct of survival. That's the reason children tend to be jealous, ambitious and egoistic. This is the reason that we, as parents and care givers, should observe and analyze all their actions to be ready to help them by correcting their wrong doings, and showing the right path based on a scale of values that will help them through the process.

Kids should know how far they can go, but they also should have the opportunity to express their needs and desires; yet, they should be aware that their desires must be based on the regulations designed for the well-being of the family in general. This way, an environment of respect, comprehension and consideration would be the norm.

However, it's well known that kids won't give up all together. They will try throughout their developmental stages to have their own way. As I already said, I had four children, but each one of them was different than the other, which is common to every family. Some of them were easy to handle, but some were not. Yet, I always made sure that the house rules were respected.

My rules were mainly based on issues that would lead them to be successful in the development of personal relationships, based on loving God over all things, and their neighbors, as they love themselves. Another rule was don't do to others, what you don't want others to do you. This teaching would help kids to develop respect to other people in general. And not only this, they will learn to have consideration with people that are different from them.

For this to take place at home, I made sure that my kids respected one another no matter their age. You may be surprised if I tell you that every now and then, some conflict would come up; but it would not last long because there I was as a referee to help them solve the situation before it became a war, making sure that justice was established.

An example of this was the following: When one of my sons was four, his brother, who at the time was thirteen, went to watch TV with him because his TV set was out of order. I was in the kitchen fixing dinner when I heard them arguing. I dropped what I was doing and showed up at the scene and asked:

"What's going on here? Then the little one said: "I'm mad because I want to see my programs and he wants to watch his, and this is not his TV."

Can you see the degree of selfishness on the part of this kid? That is how kids are. But there I was ready to establish justice. I turned off the TV and asked him: "Is this your TV? How much did you pay for it?" "Make some deals, otherwise you won't watch anything."

I went back to the kitchen and they were watching a program together. After a while, I returned to the room and asked them: "Is everything okay?"

Then the little one said: "Yes Mommy; we decided that he is going to watch one of my programs with me, and then we'd watch one of his. We are going to take turns" I always enforce the idea that our rights end, where the next persons' rights begin. My children took this so seriously that they have always shown respect for others.

Another key point I want to discuss is that for kids to comprehend the meaning of being considerate, their parents and or care givers, should set an example. We need to recognize that they have some rights, being one of them to receive an explanation for any command or recommendation given. I have heard parents giving their kids an order, and when they ask why, they say: "Because I say so!"

I consider this an incorrect answer because I don't think is disrespectful for them to know the intention behind an order, or a suggestion. If parents and or care givers would be in the disposition of explaining the issue, what so ever it may be, this would help them think and evaluate any action on their part, and the educational process would be easier. This way they would start discerning and evaluating what they hear, and they would be more receptive to the good intention behind the advice.

The following is a simple example of what I mean. When my kids started jumping on the bed, I used to tell them not to do it because two things could happen: either they might fall off the bed and break some bones, which would make them hurt a lot and I would have to take them to the hospital; or the bed will break, and I would have to go to the furniture store to buy a new one, and there would be less money for the family needs; including toys. This method really worked for me.

But even though we try to do the right thing, it may get to the point that we may think we have lost control. Sometimes, I also felt frustrated because kids do not give up. On every developmental stage, they would try to find their own ways. But what should be our position in dealing with it? Firmness of character.

We should never allow our kids to have their own ways. I'm not saying that this is an easy task. The following is an example of how I dealt with a little thief. When my youngest son was only four years old, he came home eating an icy he bought at a candy store near the house, and when I asked him where did he get the money from? He said: "I found it." When I asked him where? He said: "In Daddy's drawer." Even though I scolded him several times for doing that, he repeated the action. But I had to be firm so he would stop doing this. And I said to him: "Listen to me, you have become a thief and thieves go to jail." When I said this, he got very worried and said: "No Mommy, I don't want to go to jail."

Then I told him not to do this anymore because now he takes a nickel, later he may take a quarter, then a dollar and so on. And you would get to a point of becoming a thief, and thieves go to jail. And you know what? Ever since, if he wanted to buy something, he asked for the money. He would not even take a penny without permission. Some of the strategies I used to mold my children's character, for some people were, somehow, drastic; nevertheless, my children appreciate me for doing that. And they have used some of my strategies with their kids and are reaping good fruit.

Another crucial point I want to present is the importance to raise kids to be trustworthy. At my house, lying was not permitted. For this to take place we, adults, should set the example. It is sad to say, but many parents lie to their kids. Do not promise them what is not going to be fulfilled; otherwise they would lose confidence altogether. Neither lie to other people in front of them. How could we enforce truthfulness, if we are the first one to lie?

My kids learned not to lie at an early age even if they felt they would be punished. One strategy I used was telling them that truth is only one thing; if you tell the truth, no matter how much time has gone by, you would always say the same thing; but if you tell a lie, later on you may say something different, because what you have said has slipped off your mind, and this could get you in trouble.

I also told them that if sometimes they tell the truth, but another time they lie, I would lose confidence in them and I won't believe them at all. Yet, if they did the wrong thing and they told me about it, I was careful not to jump on them right away. I listened to them to evaluate what had happened and told them how to avoid making the same mistake in the future. I realized that if I was too harsh when they confessed their wrong doing, they would not open their heart any more. My children have shown me how well they learned this rule. The following incident is an example of what I'm saying.

When one of my sons was ten years old, my husband had some bananas in a sack to be ripen. My son didn't know there were bananas in the sack, so he climbed on it to get something that was on the top shelf of a closet. My youngest son was only eight months old, but he was already walking and climbing, so when my husband saw the bananas all mashed up, he blamed it on the baby. But my son said to him: "Oh, no, it wasn't the baby; it was me. I didn't know there were bananas in there"

The baby could have carried the blame because he could not talk yet. Nevertheless, he was so honest, that told the truth.

Another one of my rules was making my children aware of the reason we were going to the stores. This way they learned that not every time I went shopping, I had to buy toys. It's very disgusting to see children at the shopping mall throwing tantrums because they want something from the store that their parents are no in the position of buying at the time. Yet, my youngest son tried to make me buy a toy rifle that he saw at the supermarket. When I got there, he grabbed the rifle. I told him: "You know better that I didn't come to buy toys, so put it back." But he ignored me and continued walking behind me with the rifle. When I got to the cashier, I told her the rifle was not part of my shopping.

There was a lady by the cashier that said: "Poor thing, he wants the rifle." Then I told the lady: "Poor of me if I buy it because it was clear from the beginning that I didn't come to buy toys."

When the cashier finished, the bagging guy carried the shopping to my car. When my son saw me going to the car, he ran back to the place where he got it, and put it back, and got in the car.

Although he was acting like this, he was not crying because he knew better than that. He was just trying to see if I would give up. If I would have followed his constant and firm desires, I would have lost the battle.

Children need to know that when we say no, it means no. If they discover that they could get what they want by insisting, they will become dissatisfied beings, always struggling for more, no matter how much they have acquired. This is the reason we as parents and care givers, should be aware of this in order to educate children to be matured beings, able to handle life using wisdom; knowing that we cannot have what we want, all the time.

Something else I consider very important is making sure that our children are in a safe place all times. They should be aware of who to be with at school, as well as on the playground. When I was raising my kids, the school environment in my neighborhood was safe, but every now and then, there were sad cases on the news from other places; so, I was concerned about it, because it could happen there too.

This is the reason for me to deal with a situation one of my sons provoked when he was in kindergarten. One day his teacher was absent, and the students were dismissed. My kid, instead of going to his aunt's house who was his babysitter, he went to one of his classmate's house without permission. When his aunt noticed other kids from the neighborhood returning home, she started to wonder where he would be. Then she asked one of the kids if he had seen my son, and he told her where he was.

When I went to pick him up, his aunt told me about the incident. At that moment, I didn't say anything to him; but when we got home, I said to him: "Listen son, do you know why this should never happen again? Let's say that someone comes and takes you away from school. Your aunt may think that you are in your friend's house. This way that person would have enough time to take you to a faraway place. And by the time we realize you are not with your friend, it would be too late." Believe you me, this never happened again. Sometimes we need to exaggerate in order to get our kids' attention. I personally used these types of strategies to help my children understand life issues.

I entitled this chapter "A Crucial Age" because the stage from birth to six years of age is the foundation on which character starts to develop. This is the importance of making sure their physical and emotional needs are fulfilled on daily basis. This stage, depending on how they are treated, will help them develop a well-defined personality.

As I initiated this chapter, I mentioned how many animal species treat their pups, which I consider a contrast to the way humans, who are rational beings, treat their offspring. They have lost the initiative to raise them in a normal way because, as I said before, the life issues we face now a days, prevent many parents from taking care of their children in a normal way.

My advice is that even though both parents work out side, they should make sure they find a little time to talk and listen to their kids, so they feel they are loved and secured. This must be enforced, since this is the way that would take us to raise matured children in every sense. Children with healthy mind in healthy body.

Nevertheless, it is important to know that this project is not an easy one, and we may sometimes get to a point to feel that we are wasting our time. But even though you feel this way, you should not give up. I also thought I had lost the battle. But as time went by, I noticed that by being constant and firm, plus loving and understanding, little by little, I was creating in my kids a positive effect. When they became teenagers, they showed me I did not waste my time. They let me know that my intention was correct.

Keep on being firm and constant with relation to the values to enforce, but overall, loving and affectionate. This way the goal to develop your children's character would be accomplished.

Chapter IV
A New Challenge, Let's Face It

The term challenge may provoke in the reader a sense of struggle. In the previous chapter I presented information on how to deal with the first stage of the child, which I also consider to be a challenge. But the process doesn't end there.

From six to twelve years of age, children's interests start to change. During this period, school environment and playground become great threat that they will face; but this also becomes a challenge to the parents. I know how frustrating it is the mission of leading children through the right path on which they have to deal with conflicts between what is right and what is wrong.

One of them is the conflicts they may encounter between the values taught at home, and what they are exposed to at school. It may get to the point to feel admiration for one of their classmates or a playground partner, which may tempt them to follow what they say or do, because, for some kids, what friends say or do sometimes weights more than what parents and teachers say.

When my oldest son entered school, he came home using a word in Spanish with the incorrect pronunciation. When I asked him why he was saying the word incorrectly, he said:

"I think that's the way it should be said because at school everybody says it this way." This incident proofs how important is for them what other kids do or say.

This is the reason we should be aware of every movement, and ready to correct any wrong doing, be it the way they talk or how they act, so it would not become a habit. Yet, be also ready to praise them for good or improved conduct. We must not forget that they are still in the process of developing their personality and this will bring up their esteem. I have noticed that good conduct many times is ignored.

During this stage, they start to watch and admire public figures such as sport players, artists, musicians, actors and actresses, that many times become their heroes. They may dream of becoming one of them, and there's nothing wrong with that, if their scale of values is based on principles which are favorable to the social and emotional development of the child.

Our responsibility should be to re-enforce those virtues we were trying to instill in them during the first stage, and at the same time, we should start preparing them to face the next stage which is adolescence.

One of those virtues has to do with being responsible; and a good sign of responsibility has to do with punctuality. The following incident is a personal action which may be considered out of the norm, but it is an example of how I handled it.

When my youngest son was in the sixth grade, he asked me to move him from the school in our neighborhood, to an elementary school near the high school where I was working. So, I did. But we needed to leave the house earlier to drop him at his school, so I would get to my school in time. For a few days I had a hard time trying for him to be in the car. Then I said to him: "Next time this happens, I'm going to take off and leave you behind."

He probably thought I was joking, and the next day was the same situation. I blew the car horn three times, and it seemed he was ignoring it. Then I took off and left him in the house. But don't think it was easy for me. I spent the whole day thinking about it.

"Oh, my "God, I shouldn't have done this." But I also said to myself: "I don't care. This may be the way he would learn to be responsible."

To add to my bothersome situation, when I returned home, he approached me with the following complain: "Mommy, today I had three tests." And I said:

"Oh yes; but you are going to have three Fs, because you don't have an excuse for not attending school today."

Would you like to know what was the outcome of this episode? I developed a very responsible human being. From then on, I didn't have to deal with the situation. He would get up on his own, got dress and had breakfast in time. And was in the car at the right time. But let me tell you that I was able to do this because he was not going to be home by himself. This is just my experience. I should mention that when he started to work, his first evaluation surprised him because he had a 105 %. He got extra points for the way he presented himself, the way he treated people and his punctuality.

My personal observation is that too much tolerance may be providing the stage for many kids and teenagers to be out of control. I was firm and constant. If I said I was going to do something, so I did. This way they realized that when I said something, I meant it. But at the same time, I was willing to have a friendly conversation with them, letting them know that what so ever I did to get their attention was out of my interest in helping them to become good citizens, capable of dealing with life issues with wisdom.

But I also let them know that when they reach their adulthood, no matter their actions, good or bad, would be their own responsibility. Yet, I also put emphasis on what is the outcome for being people of virtue. In other words what so ever they sow, they would reap. I took those chances because I had established a good relationship with them from birth. Otherwise, it, probably, would have been harder to accomplish my goal.

The development of good social relationships is another important issue to bring to the table. When children reach school age, they should be capable of sharing with other kids; but we should be ready to follow up on them, because now they are going to be exposed to kids with different personalities.

One strategy I used was to allow my kids to bring home who they considered a friend. In the back yard we had a basketball ring and their friends came to play basketball there. They also had a Nintendo and other passive games, plus Television. In fact, they were equipped to make their friends welcome home. They were treated with kindness, so they felt accepted and respected.

The objective of this strategy was for me to have the opportunity to know who their friends were. Their friends also showed respect to us in every aspect. This had to do with the advice I gave my kids since they were very young. I told them to show their friends that our home rules had to be respected.

They took this so seriously, that even if they were home by themselves, the rules were kept, something that surprised my neighbor who expressed it this way: "You don't know how much I admire your sons, because even if you are not home, when their friends come to be with them, everything feels so calm. I don't see or hear anything out of control."

There is something else I want to present, which I consider necessary in the mission of guiding children towards the development of a good character. I think that they need to be aware of what is going on in the neighborhood, be it good or bad. They should also be aware of the outcomes of bad behavior, and the satisfaction they would experience by doing the right thing.

Getting them to observe and analyze the harsh and sad situations some young guys are going through for not doing the right thing, could be a good method; but don't ignore that they need to have follow up through the process.

At this point, comes to my mind some sad examples of some families, that in order to raise their kids to become perfect guys, made the mistake of overprotecting them. Their mothers took them to school every morning and watched them until they entered the classroom. They were picked up after school and taken home. They were not allowed to go out at all. They were forbidden to hang out with friends with the good intention of keeping them from getting influenced by other kids.

But when they became teenagers, since the middle school was not closed to their homes, they were on their own. And it is painful to say that these guys got out of their parents' hands. One of them finished high school and went to college, where he met a girlfriend who happened to be a drug addict, and he ended up as one of them, creating a very difficult situation to the family. The others also became drug addicts, and one of them ended up in jail.

These have been a sad experience for those parents for trying, with very good intentions, to protect their sons. If they would have been aware that overprotecting them was going to be counterproductive, I know things would have been different.

Our children need to know about common life issues, and guided to develop wisdom, so they would be able to handle daily situations in a way that would allow them to make the correct decisions. And remember that if they feel their parents did not take their time to train them in the way they should go, they will show resentment towards them.

Several of my students confessed to me why they were behaving the way they did. Some of them thought they were just scolded in a tough manner, without letting them express their feelings. Others said their parents were so busy working and taking care of their own business, that they felt they didn't care about them, at all. This is the importance of being aware of their attitude, in order to see if there is something provoking that attitude; but willing to deal with it.

My advice to parents and other people in charge of kids, is not to get discouraged if they feel it is too hard to deal with them. My experience as a teacher, proved me, that even if the kids are already out of control, it's never too late to start the process of molding their lives. Just keep in mind that the affectionate need of our children is a must in dealing with their conduct.

Another trick is to listen to them. They may have some issues they would like to discuss, but if we don't show them confidence, they may try to find answers in the wrong place, which could be counterproductive. And don't forget that if the child feels loved and respected, he/she would, little by little, learn to respond the same way.

Chapter V
The Challenge Is Still On; Be On the Alert

When children get to be thirteen years old, they have reached a very difficult stage which is adolescence. The term adolescence has a Spanish connotation which is to suffer pain. This stage is the transition towards adulthood; which could be painful for them because at this stage, they are not quite adults, neither small kids. They sometimes may act as little children, and you could hear commends like this: "Look; that child thinks he/she is still a little kid." But if they act as adults, the comment may be: "Look; that child thinks he/she is already a man/woman." This is the reason parents and caregivers need to be aware of this, so they would be able to face this new challenge with wisdom.

It's imperative to find ways to establish a good relationship with children, making sure that, our intentions are backed up by the way we, as adults, conduct ourselves. Being aware of how difficult it is for adolescents to deal with life issues, whoever is in charge of them, needs to observe them on a daily basis, and if there is a sign of disappointment, or disgust, leave them alone for a while; but when you feel they are relaxed, and willing to hold a conversation, approach them in a way that they would consider to be out of love, so they would understand that your intentions are for their wellbeing.

Remember that they are going through the process of getting to know who they are. It is our responsibility to help them consider themselves as respected and valuable human beings. Avoid using words that could lower their esteem. Words are powerful. If you feel oral communication is not possible, writing them a note exposing your intentions, could be a solution. And as I already expressed, be aware of any good deed on their part and praise them. It is sad to say, but many times children's good behavior is overlooked.

There is something else I consider crucial in the development of the character of the children which is how they manage their social life. One aspect of this has to do with the way they choose their friends. This is the reason for me to I allowed my children to bring their friends home since they were very young, and this way I became aware of who their friends were.

If by any chance, one of them would stop coming, I asked them why; and they, sadly said: "Mommy, he's doing something that isn't according to our values." My kids were able to respond this way, because they already knew the difference between what is right and what is wrong; and the outcomes of both. If kids are conscious of this, they would evaluate what they see their friends doing, and would avoid following what they do, if by any chance, is something that would lead them through the wrong path.

Although my kids had permission to bring their friends home, the time arrived, when I had to make the decision to allow them to explore and get acquainted with the outside environment. This was really something worrisome, because the environment had change for the bad, due to drug abuse, and the result of this habit which had become a social problem in the community.

When my oldest son turned thirteen years old, came to me asking permission to go to his friend's house. This friend of his, used to come to our house every afternoon to spend time with my son. Even though I was hesitant, I let him go; but I specified it was for just an hour. He went to his visit, and two or three minutes to the hour, he was back. When I saw him, I praised him with the following words: "You've proven me that I can trust you."

From that day on, they started to share the time this way: one day his friend came to our house, and the next day, my son went to his house. This happened for some time. But, one afternoon, he asked me if he could go with his friend to play basketball at the community basketball court. This was hard for me to decide, since as I said before, right there was one of the places where bad things were taking place. But I started to think this way: "He is already an adolescent; if I don't allow him to go, he may become rebellious, and will try to find the way to do it any way, against my will."

Then I rely on the set of values I've instilled in him from birth, and asked him: "Do you think you are going to feel comfortable spending time there?" And he responded this way: "I just want to play some basketball." Then I said: "I'm going to let you go, but if you see anything that looks out of the norm, take off."

They went there three days in a roll, but the third day, when my son came back, he talked to me and said: "You know Mommy? You were right. I really understand your worry about me going there. I won't go there anymore"

Three days later, my son came to me and said: "Mommy, do you know what happened at the basketball court yesterday? The police came and whoever was there had a hard time. Mommy, good thing I was not there."

This is the reason parents or care givers have the responsibility to establish in children a set of values that would help them in the process of becoming good adults in every aspect. As my kids were growing up, I started to give them certain degree of freedom, but it was conditional. This provided them the opportunity to get to know the environment; and this way, I could evaluate how they were handling that freedom. It was my obligation to guide them through the processes.

When my sons turned fifteen years old, they started to hang around the neighborhood with some friends, after they returned from school, but they were to come back before six o' clock, the time we had supper. A few minutes before six, they were back home. Even after becoming adults, (since I had them at home for a long time) they submitted to my rules.

One of the strategies I used was telling them that the time for me to go a bed was 10:30 pm; and it was not fare for me not to have a good night sleep thinking where my sons might be, to get up early in the morning to go to work, to earn the money to support the family. This rule they kept without any fuss.

Molding Lives

My oldest son was so conscious of this rule, that even after coming back from the NAVY where he spent four and a half years of his life, if he was not coming home for the night, he let me know, so I would not worry. At the time, he was already a twenty-three years old man. This is what I have been trying to emphasize from the beginning: we must, at any age, establish the foundation on which our children would build their character. This way they would learn how to make the correct decision, not because they are afraid of being punished, but because they know the outcomes of being matured.

There is something sad I would like to repeat, which have to do with the way some parents, with good intention, have decided to keep their children at home or locked in the yard, not allowing them to see what is going on around them; and even forbidding them from having friends because they are afraid their kids get out of control, and at the end have suffered the deception of seeing them taking the wrong path.

Another comment which I consider we should give some thought is that some parents try to enforce good behavior by using outrageous means of authority, thinking this is the right way, without showing their children love and understanding. They neither give them something to substitute for what has been forbit, neither show them a clear picture of what is going on around the neighborhood.

These children may probably submit to their rules, but not by being conscious of the importance of them, but by being afraid of the punishment. To be scared may be something superficial, but to be aware of the lesson they could learn by observing the rules of life in a mature way, is powerful.

And repeating myself; it is very important to let children and young adults observe what so ever is going on outside, and the consequences of not submitting to the rules of life, and the great satisfaction of being good citizens. Otherwise, they will end up facing serious situations for not having the correct tools to handle life issues.

This takes me to a story my Mom told my sisters and me, when we were little girls, probably with the intention of teaching us to respect other people's belongings. She said that there was a mother who had a little boy who used to steal eggs from the neighborhood, and when he got home, she cooked them and they ate them together. Later, he started to steal chicken, then he stole a pig, later a cow. She was taking advantage of the free food supply without realizing that sooner or later something drastic would happen to her son.

So, when he became an adult, he continued to be a thief, but this time, he really got in trouble, because trying to rob a man, he happened to kill him, and ended up being sentenced to the electric chair. When he was asked to say what was his last desire, he said to kiss his Mom. She was brought to him and when she put her face in the position to receive the kiss, he bit her cheek.

Everyone got furious for that action; but when he was asked to give the reason for doing that, he said: "I did it because she is the one who should be in my position because as a child, when I started to steal eggs, later animals from the neighborhood she cooked them and we enjoyed the food together. She never took her time to correct my wrong doing."

My mother's intention behind the story was to let us know that it was her responsibility to be aware of our behavior and to be ready to correct any wrong doing in time, so it would not become a habit.

Being alert, and willing to do something about it, if something out of the norm goes on, is very much appreciated by children. My kids have expressed how much they admire me for the way I dealt with their behavior. When children feel good about the way they are doing at school or at their job, they really appreciate their parents for having taken their time to guide them through the right path.

When a child feels proud of their parents, they will try to avoid them to suffer. This brings me to a situation my youngest son had to face when he was only thirteen years old. At the time, I was working at a job that prevented me from being at home to receive my boy after school. This means he had enough time to be on his own until 7:00 o' clock in the evening.

One evening, when I got home, he came to me and told me that some of his classmates wanted him to hang around with them; but he told them that he won't go out without my permission. At this point they started to make fun of him calling him mama's boy, fool, silly boy. He said to me that he felt an eager to go with them; but he won't do it because he knew if something would happen to him, I was going to suffer, and he did not want me to suffer.

And as usual, I was ready to praise him for that, but added that, I knew I was going to suffer, but he was going to suffer even more, because I have always said that if any of my children would get in trouble for being where they are not supposed to be, or doing the wrong thing, I was going to let them suffer the consequences till the end. If for this kid my feelings were not important, he would have listened to them.

A few month later he came to me and told me that those kids that were asking him to hang out with them at that time, broke into a school and were sent to a correctional institution. Then he said: "Oh my God, Mommy, if I would have been with them, now I would have been in great trouble."

During this stage, kids also start to get interested on sexual issues. If they were not oriented on how to deal with this matter, they may end up being parents before the correct time. Or may also end up with a sexual transmitted disease. For this reason, it is important to be prepared to talk to them openly. Although it may sound silly or funny, youngsters should be aware that abstinence is the best method to avoid such problems. This brings me to a situation my grandson experience with relation to this issue.

He was ridiculed by his friends because even at his twenty-four years old, the age he got married, he had never had sex. But this is how he reacted, according to what he told me. He said he told them, that he had not wasted his time, because this way he did not have to worry about getting a girl pregnant, neither getting infested with any sexually transmitted disease.

The modern trend of experimenting sex before being ready for it, has created a very sad situation; I dare to express myself this way because there are too many little children being victims of it; something that could have been avoided. And the saddest thing is that those youngsters that become parents are also victims of their mistakes because they have to deal with the responsibility of being parents.

Many parents are providing their kids artificial methods that are not 100% safe, and this may also provoke the same situation. This is the reason I insist that parents should take time to educate their youngsters on this matter.

However, I know how difficult it is for some parents to deal with the subject. I should confess that for me was difficult to approach my older kids with this subject. For the youngest was a little easier. Nevertheless, although I did not get to the deep point of the subject, I would give them certain advice on how to deal with this matter. I always told them that no matter how a girl would approach them, to respect them, because some day they may have a girl, and I knew they would not tolerate any one who would abuse her.

Something we, as parents, should do is to let our kids know that we are willing to listen to them, so they could express their feelings and worries with confidence. This tactic helped my youngest son to deal with a temptation he faced. When he was in the seventh grade, he told me that a classmate, approached him, opened her blouse and showed him her breast; but he just turned his head, and ignored her. I praised him for behaving this way and told him that probably she was just looking for a little affection.

When my sons became teenagers, I told them not to be with a girlfriend in a lonely place to avoid temptation. And I also made them aware that if by any chance, they got a girl pregnant, I would force them to be responsible for the baby, even if they have no choice but to get a part time job to support the baby. And I enforced the idea of becoming fathers the correct way, rather than by an accident.

I also advice my sons to avoid getting in love until they would be ready to get marry. So as teen, they were surrounded by girls, and shared with them as a group, but no compromise.

The following story proves what I am trying to say: I was sent to work at a school in which one of my neighbor's daughter was a student. This teenage girl started to visit us in the evenings, but a few weeks later she gave me a compliment for the way one of my sons dealt with her. She confessed to me that the reason she was visiting us was because she liked my son so much that had fallen in love with him; but he was so respectful and serious, that told her he was not into that yet because he wanted to concentrate on his college work and would not have time for her.

What really surprised her, as she expressed, was how respectful he was. She also said that another guy would have just fooled around with her and later would have dropped her; but my son acted like a serious man.

Another incident that proves how well my method related to this issue worked is the following:

When my youngest son entered high school, at the end of the school year, he got home with a present and a greeting card signed by a group of female students. The next school year I was sent to that same high school to work, and when I called attendance, I noticed that some of the names I saw in the greeting card my son received, were there.

I asked one of the girls if she knew Giovannie, and she asked me: "Do you know him?" Then I told her he was my son. When I asked her why they have treated him in such a way; she said: "Ms. Gotay, we really did it because we were eager to have a friend who would respect us, and that was your son." When this girl told the other girls that I was his mother, all of them came and gave me the same remark. They really appreciated the wonderful time they had with his company. They told me I should really be very proud of him. They admired me for the son I raised.

Although, for some of their peers, my kids were considered silly for not taking advantage of certain opportunities that were against their scale of values, they were following my advice. I trained them to ignore people's opinion because what really matters was how they felt about themselves.

I want to aboard the following subject that has to do with children's decision making. This is a delicate subject, because many parents are the ones who make their decisions of what profession or trait, their kids should go for; which many times is against what their kids want, something that may be disappointing for them, and they may develop a sense of disgust.

Many youngsters get to high school and do not have any goal already set in mind. This may be due to lack of information. Parents should help their children decide what profession or career they would like to go for; but the decision should be according to their abilities. I am not referring only to a profession from a university, which will take them from four to eight years to graduate. There are quite a few careers such as computer technology, beautician, dental assistant, medical assistant, auto-mechanic, electrician, plumber, and other traits that offer good positions.

My advice is that if parents notice that their children are showing an ability or a specific talent, help them to concentrate on it. Encourage them to find information about it and to follow their desires.

I know a case of a father who observe that his child had the ability to draw and color pictures in such a way, that he encouraged him to go to an interview. There were quite a few candidates, but he was chosen among all of them. He was very successful in the job. If his father would have ignored him, this would have never happened. That was one side of the coin.

Now, the other side of the coin is this: I know a lady who had a son that did such a great job at the university, that he got a very good job offer in the USA, but his mother prevented him from accepting the job because she did not want to see him gone away. This proves how different people are. You could see that for some people, letting the youngsters find their way to deal with their life is normal; for others it is having them near. To me the correct way should be letting them find their way through independence. But I should state that if we have given them a good foundation, there is nothing to fear.

An experience I had with relation to this matter was the following: When my oldest son was in the tenth grade, he came to me and asked me to take him out of school because he wanted to join a program that was developed to help the drop out students. The tittle of the program was Job Corp. This program was designed to prepare the students for the GED (high school equivalence test) and provided the opportunity to have a trait.

This petition for me was a little harsh to accept, since I was a teacher in the same school district in Puerto Rico, and what would others think about me? I talked to him and explained him that this program was not for him, but for students that have lost interest in school. Then he said that he was tired of the school routine.

"Okay", I said; and the next day I went to his school to dismiss him. When I got there, the principal of that school, whom the previous school year was the principal of the school where I worked, heard of my intention, asked me if I had become crazy. And I said: "No, Sir, I'm not crazy, but probably my son is. This is what he wants, and this is what he gets. What so ever the outcome, it's his. This way he cannot blame me if things do not go alright."

The day came for him to be at the new school. At first everything seemed to be okay. But a few weeks later he came to me and said: "Mommy, you were right, this is not for me." Then I said: "I knew I was right, but I wanted you to know it for yourself. Now you have no choice but to start the tenth grade all over again, which you were almost finished."

A few weeks later he came to me very excited and asked me: "Mommy, can you give me $2.50 every day? I heard about a school in Humacao, that is offering a course to prepare drop out students for the GED, and I want to take advantage of this."

I said: "It is okay with me. He registered, and faithfully went to that school. He took the GED test and had a very good score. He came home very happy for his achievement. But he gave me another shock. He said: "Don't think I'm going to college." My response was: "You know son what I've always said to you and your siblings, that your decisions, good or bad, are your decisions. Yet, the outcomes good or bad, are yours, too."

Well, Mommy, I have decided to join the US Army." No problem. If that is your decision, it is fine with me. He went and took the test to enlist in the USA Army and did so well, that was able to join the US NAVY in which spent four and a half years. When he came out of it, he got married. He also registered in college and attended it for two years; but stopped going because he was trying to be in the buying and selling cars business, which really was not successful. He tried other jobs, but finally he decided to go back to college which has given him the opportunity of having a very good and rewarding job.

Don't think my son was problematic for the way he was acting. He was always respectful and willing to let me know his ideas. He knew I was not controlling him; I gave him the opportunity to use the skill of trying and error, until he got to the place he is. Now a days, we are proud of one another.

This story may sound wrong to those who think that parents should take control of their children's decision. But I know of cases in which parents have decided their kids' profession and they are not happy. And some have even gotten away from their parents, so they would have freedom of choice. As I had already expressed, if a parent notices a specific ability in one of his/her kids, is good to give a suggestion, in opposition to forcing them.

The idea of presenting my oldest son story is to let the reader know that we, as parents, should allow our children to demonstrate that they have developed a set of values, and that they are aware of the results for not abiding by them. We can see that even though my son, apparently, was out of control, he showed that he had a good relationship with me, his mother, and how much confidence he had in me, to express his ideas and objectives.

You could also observe, the way he moved around trying to find ideas and alternatives to his inquiries, and the way he moved around trying to find stability. When my son joined the US Navy, I had to deal with a conflict of opinion. But I said: "Well, I think he is matured enough to choose what he wants to do and also to handle what he would encounter over there." And as I already expressed, he went there, came back and is doing beautifully.

Many children do not feel comfortable to express their feelings or preoccupations to their parents, because their parents have not shown them enough confidence. They are afraid to be misunderstood. As I said before, parents have the challenge of inquiring what profession or trait their children would like to pursue and be ready to assist them in the process to accomplish it.

Children, while playing, may be suggesting their interest in a career. If you notice that your children are showing an ability in some specific skill or talent, try to encourage them, making sure that it is really what they want to do.

My advice to parents is to encourage their children to be aware that they need to be prepared to face the future; but they should be allowed to make their own decision for what they would like to do.

I think that if you are doing a job you are not comfortable with, the production would not be the best.

When my oldest son decided to join the US Navy, I had to deal with a family conflict because my Mom almost dropped dead when she found out her favorite grandson had made that decision. But I told her: "Listen Mommy, I think he was matured enough to have taken that decision. If that's what he wanted to do, he has my approval.

He went and came back. He went through a course of life, that I know taught him some lessons. Who knows, if I would have interfered with his decision, things for the both of us would have been different.

As I expressed in one of the previous chapters, if we observe most of the animals, we will see how well they care for their offspring. They care for them in a very good manner. They are fed, protected from any danger, and even entertained; but at the same time, they train them to be on their own. Yet, many times this treatment has been ignored by the human beings.

Kids need to be trained to be independent, so they would be able to handle life challenges in a matured manner. Now a days many children are so attached to their parents, and this has created a sense of insecurity. They may feel frustrated, because they have not had the opportunity to grow emotionally. If we as parents, have established the principles that would guide our children in the process of becoming matured beings, we would live peacefully, because they would stay away from trouble.

I thank God for giving me the tools to deal with such a very delicate project of molding the life of each of my children. And not only this, but He also guided me to deal with my students in a way that I was respected and admired by them. He guided me in the mission of training my kids in the way they should go. I was firm and constant in dealing with them; but I always explained them the reason for my demands.

My kids were admired for the way they behaved, to the point, that I was asked several times, how did I raise my kids in such an environment, in which so many youngsters had become drug addicts and my kids did not. And I told them that I claimed wisdom from God, so I could establish some rules and regulations to help my children to become matured beings.

This prayer was answered right away, because I started to establish a set of clear rules and regulations and a set of rewards for good deeds, and some sanctions for not doing what they were supposed to do. But at the same time, I asked for patience and understanding, so we would be able to enjoy a good mother-children relationship.

Something else I did was not to judge anybody's kids, if they started to take the wrong path. I felt very sorry for them and included them in my prayer. Through my life I have seen, that some parents have judged the neighbors' kids; and when their kids became teenagers, at least one of them got into the same situation, or even worst. It is a very bad habit to waste our precious time minding other people's kids business, instead of concentrating in dealing with their own kids' matters. We should not judge, not to be judged.

In summary, if we are constant and firm with relation to our rules of conduct, which should be based on the moral and spiritual values which are so necessary for the development of a good character, we would be able to experience a great satisfaction for seeing our children dealing with life issues in a matured manner. "SO, DON'T EVER GIVE UP!"

Chapter VI
Words Shape Up Realities

This chapter is based on a work I had to turn in while taking a course for the endorsement of my English teaching certificate, so I would be certified to teach ESOL, which stands for English to Speakers of Other Languages. The subject impacted me so much that I decided to include it in this work.

If we, as citizens, would understand how powerful words are, the world would be a paradise. Words have the power of affecting us in a positive and/or in a negative way. The development of our personality depends mostly, on the words we have heard from birth. That is the reason of being very careful of any message we are trying to send our children. They need to hear words that bring their self-esteem up, so they would respond the same way. Yet, we need to be aware that this is a challenge we must face along their developmental stages.

It is sad to say, but many children, as they become teenagers, feel so disgusted, that cannot find satisfaction in life. Nothing motivates them to set goals, so they do not really know what their future life would be like. If children hear words that denigrate their character from an early age, they would feel unworthy. But, on the other hand, if they feel appreciated and respected; but guided with wisdom through the process of becoming mature beings, things would be different. If we, parents and/or caregivers, let them know how much appreciated they are to us, they will give us great surprises. And how would they recognize our good intentions? By the words we use. Words have weigh and measurement. (Literal translation of a Spanish saying.)

The following is a real example of what I am trying to say. My father once opened his heart and told me how much suffering his father caused him, for being different than other young guys in the neighborhood. He seemed to be withdrawn and shy since he was a little boy. And when he became a teenager, trying for him to behave like other young guys in their neighborhood, his father used words that denigrated his character. He wanted him to hang out with friends, to drink alcoholic beverages and to go out with women.

But my father was a thinker. He really enjoyed observing nature. He admired the beautiful world a magnificent being has created. Although my father was a very talented person, his low esteem prevented him from becoming a more successful person.

Many parents have failed to have a good parent-child relationship because of the way they have tried to correct their children. Words have power. If children feel mistreated and disrespected, when they become adults, they may end up getting far away from that environment. Or they may become shy, insecure or introverted people.

Through the thirty-three years I worked as a teacher, I was able to see many students improved their conduct, because of the words I used. I used words that took them to auto-exam themselves, so they realized the reason I had for any means of correction. But I also oriented them on how to improve their conduct.

We need to be aware that from birth, children go through a learning process that would make them capable of facing adulthood. Therefore, we must observe all their actions in order to praise the good and correct the ones that are out of the norm; but not forgetting that words shape up realities.

However, there may be cases in which a child that was mistreated and put down by using nasty words, when reaching his/her adulthood, he/she had done a great work. But this does not have to be this way, because by the time this person overcomes all this situation, he/she had suffered a lot.

An example of this is the following story: I know a woman, that as a child suffered by the way her mother referred to her since she was a child. In an effort of seeing her being more alert, she expressed about her as follows: "You are stupid, and silly. You are worth for nothing. I wonder what your life will be in the future."

This treatment made this woman considered herself exactly what her Mom said about her for many years. But she surprised many people for the way she succeeded. She went to college and became a very successful teacher. She also became a very talented person. She can sing, play the guitar, write songs and poems. She is also the author of some books. However, if she would have had a better treatment as a child, her life would have been happier and more rewarding. It really took her many years to get to where she is now.

As I previously said, words can affect us in a positive, and/or a negative way. The cases presented above, are examples of negative treatment. Now, let me present cases in which positive words; I mean words that would create in the listener, a sense of security, understanding and above all, love.

My youngest child, when he was only eight years old, due to his parents' divorce, for some time he became a little problematic. He started to feel mad, mean and outspoken; he also lowered his grades. But what really worried me was that he boasted several times he was a bad boy.

But every time I heard him expressing himself this way, I talked to him in a peaceful manner: "No, you're not a bad boy; sometimes you behave a little out of control, but you are a good boy. And remember that you are a child of God.

And little by little I was using words that would, somehow, ease the situation. I also explained to him that even though his father was no longer living with us, he will always love him, and take care of him. By talking to him, while letting him bring up his concerns, I was able to see how his feelings were changing for the best.

By the way, he happened to develop such a personality, that has been admired by girls, teachers, bosses, friends, wife and in-laws, and over all, by his parents.

Another example of how words shape up realities, is the following case. One of my tenth-grade students, when I asked him to concentrate in his work, he gave me a nasty look, and made a remark in a low voice, and I felt insulted. I ignored his action, but at the end of the class, I took him aside and asked him: "Have you ever felt I was disrespectful to you? Because if you feel this way, I ask you to forgive me." And he said: "No."

Then I said: "Yet, I feel that today you were disrespectful to me when I asked you to concentrate in your job." He apologized to me; but I took my time to instruct him on how to control his attitude, and at the same time I brought up some good things I observed in him. And believe you me, he became one of my best students.

The following story is another example of how powerful words are. One of my students at a high school I worked at in the State of Florida, from the beginning of the school year, she showed that she was disgusted. I used to stand at the classroom door to greet my students as they came in; but when I greeted this particular girl, she answered me in a disgusting way.

The next day, I greeted her again, but this time she was a little polite. The third day she was so nice that she even had a smile in her face. Then I took advantage of this and asked her if she could do me a favor, and she accepted. I sent her to take something to the school secretary.

When she returned, she asked me: "Do you really like me?" And I answered: "Why not?"

Then she said: "You know what? You are the only person who have ever liked me."

This reaction of her took me to think that the way she was behaving was probably the result of a vicious cycle. She probably was treated in a rough way, that got her to be on the defensive, which at the same time was provoking other people to avoid establishing a social relationship with her.

The story has a nice ending. This girl became a different person. Before this experience, she would come in and sat by herself. She would not communicate with any student. And after I let her know she was important to me, she became friendly with other students, and became more pleasant. She graduated from high school and went to college.

And the last of so many episodes that I experienced that had to do with how powerful words are is the following: My first experience as a high school teacher was in my country, Puerto Rico. I was sent to relieve a very experienced teacher who was going to retire that year. When I got there, the teacher told me that the homeroom students were very out of control. But she also warned me that I was going to have a very disrespectful student, and she mentioned her name. So, when I called attendant, I realized who she was.

This girl was born in the USA, but when she was in the fifth grade, her parents moved back to Puerto Rico. She was a very intelligent student, who had dominion of the English language, which was the class I taught. But due to the description the former teacher had given me about her, I made the mistake of avoiding an encounter with her. So, since she was very intelligent, and bilingual, I allowed her to sit away from the rest of the class. But the time came for her manifestation.

A few weeks after the school year started, the students entered the classroom very rowdy. Then I said: "Students, I'm going to start writing names on the board; if you see your name with two check marks next to it, your parents will receive a letter." All of them sat down quietly.

Yet, this girl moved from where she was sitting, sat next to a girl and started talking. Then I wrote her name on the board. When she saw her name there, she said: "What kind of stupid thing is that?" I added a check mark. Then she repeated the same action, so I added another check mark.

The next morning, I gave her homeroom teacher the letter for the girl to take home. When she received it, she just got out of that classroom, came to my classroom door, and said: "How long are you going to insist on this stupidity?"

And I calmly said: "Well, let me tell you that I have nothing to discuss with you; if your Mom does not come to talk to me tomorrow, you won't enter my classroom."

The next morning her mother came to see me and asked me what was the matter with her daughter, and I told her that the case was to be discussed at the principal's office. As we were walking to the office, her mother opened her heart to me and told me how difficult it had been to deal with this girl. She also said that this girl never showed affection to anybody.

When we got to the meeting, the principal asked me to express what was the situation with the student, and I said: "I prefer the student to express herself first."

When she started talking, I was shocked. She said that to me, other students were more important than she was. She accused me of ignoring her when she raised her hand, which was a lie. As I already said, she sat away from the class, and never raised her hand. I confess that the reason I let her sit where she sat and avoided to have an encounter with her was due to the warning the former teacher had given me. And since this was my first experience working with high school students, I acted that way.

But I thought that it was never too late to correct our errors, so, I expressed myself the following way: "I want to offer Victoria an apology. Although I was not aware of the way she evaluated me this is the way she has judged me. To her, this is true. Nevertheless, I'd like to say something to her, that is coming from my heart." And referring to her I said: "Do you know, Victoria that you have whatever you would need to succeed in life? You are pretty, intelligent and bilingual; however, there's something you need to deal with, and it is your attitudes. Negative attitudes will affect you, in a negative way throughout your life. If you would have come to me to let me know that you wanted to participate in class, I would have never ignored your good intention. I love to see my students taking active part in my class.

Do you want to know how powerful words are? The next day, when she saw me entering the school, she ran to me and hugged me; something that was odd in her, according to what her Mom had expressed to me that day. If I would have tried to fight back when she started to talk the way she expressed herself about me, things would have been different.

Although, according to her Mom and other of her classmates, this girl was hard to deal with, from this time on she started to be friendly. She stopped sitting away from the rest of the class and took active part in the class activities. This proof how words shape up realities.

A reality is a fact. Something genuine. But if we summarize what I have been saying related to the subject, we would realize that there are negative realities as well as positive. So, would it be possible to mold realities? Of course.

According to the examples presented in this chapter, there were negative realities as the result of negative attitudes used while dealing with the person. Yet, there were negative realities, that by the word power, changed to good realities, although the results were not seen over night.

In summary, it's very important to use positive adjectives while dealing with children, being ours, or anybody else's. I insist on the idea that to correct and educate our children, it is not necessary to use words that would make them more rebellious. Remember that words have the power to work according to our attitudes. So, let's find words to motivate our kids to behave as they should; words to help them evaluate their own behavior, and be ready to change any attitude they feel is not according to the principles we have tried to instill in them. And, at the same time, be ready to praise any good action on their part. This way they will start feeling good about themselves. And keep in mind that WORDS SHAPE UP REALITIES.

Chapter VII
The Reward For Being Firm and Constant

Some parents and care givers may feel that dealing with children conduct is a waste of time, and I don't blame anybody for feeling this way. I sometimes also felt this way. Nevertheless, I did not give up. We need to realize that dealing with children is a tough project. But, in the long run, if we have been firm and constant, but loving and understanding, we will receive the reward for that job. They will feel proud of having such responsible parents.

The way my children treat me through their years have proven me that I did not waste my time. I made my children conscious that the best gift I expect to have from them, is to show respect and consideration to me, as well as the rest of the family. I did this because when I was a girl, I observed some children who did not make their mother happy for the way they behaved, and on Mother's Day, they would come to her with a nice present. To me that was hypocrisy.

Yet, don't take me wrongly; bringing us a present is a very nice action. But I really preferred them to be respectful, responsible, honest and so on. In fact, people with good character. I also told them that to give something, not necessarily had to be on a special day. I added that if they ever see me with a financial situation or any other issue, if they are in the position of helping me out, and do it, that would be the best present of all.

My children have never forgotten this. Every time they have seen me struggling with a difficult issue, one way or another, they have helped me out. I consider them to be a blessing in my life.

One of the many rewards I have received from my children is the following: I was sent to work at a junior high school. At the meeting to open the school year, the new teachers had to introduce themselves. When I said who I was, a teacher approached me and told me about a student she had the previous year, who had my last name. When I asked her what his name was, and she told me, I said to her: "He's my son."

Then she said: "You should be very proud of such a son. I was his teacher last year, and as I observed a sixteen years old guy with such an outstanding character, I wonder, where did such a guy come from." I really felt very proud.

Another great reward I received from my oldest son. He decided to join the US NAVY. He was sent to take his training for a few months. The date he was about to finish his training, happened to be Mother's Day. He sent me a card, and when I opened it, my eyes went to a message he wrote on it that said: "To the mother who taught me how to become a man."

A few weeks after this, he had a pass to come home for a few weeks, before going to Italy.

When I asked him why he expressed himself that way in the card he said that when he observed so many of those guys who were there, so childish, not submitting to the rules and regulations. Others crying because they missed home, and things like this, and he found himself so matured, and praised by his superiors, he figured out that it had to do with the way I trained him in the way he should go.

The following story is about how some people consider all the teenagers as being irresponsible and careless. When I moved to Florida, I started to work at a school, and at the lunch room, right at the table I was sitting, some coworkers started to talk in a negative way about today's young guys. One of them said: "Today's children aren't angels." When I heard her, I said: "Let me tell you that I really have an angel home."

And she said: "You can't say that because you don't know what he does when he goes out."

I started to describe what a good relationship I had with my son. I explained to her that he is my companion. At the time, we had recently moved to Florida, and in such a short time we both are working and share the expenses in an equitable way. I also mentioned that he went out every evening just to play basketball for two hours; and sometimes to the mall to buy something. He never got home drunk, or drugged, and we were able to discuss our situations in a matured manner. Then she said: "Well, you really have an angel home." This let me know I did not waste my time as I instructed him.

Before I moved to Florida, during my summer vacations I decided to take a trip to this state. At the time, this same son of mine was seventeen, and he was going to be on his own. He was supposed to eat at his aunt's house, but he was home most of the time.

When I returned, my neighbor talked to me about how surprised she was to see that even when his friends came to spend time at the house, she never saw or heard anything out of control. She said to me: "You really have a saint as a child."

What she was not aware of was that, for me to shape up his character as a child, I had a hard time. I really had to be firm and constant, and over all full of love and understanding.

Another story that proves how important is to take the project of raising our kids seriously is the following. This same child, when he turned seventeen, joined a Basketball team, and a few weeks later the couch called me to let me know how surprised he was to see a young guy with such a good character. He said he was responsible, respectful, honest and friendly. He was specific when he mentioned that he admired the way he treated the other players.

What really surprised me is that this guy, as a child showed some characteristics that worried me. He was the one who tried to intimidate me with the Law of Child Abuse I mentioned before. This kid was outspoken and demanding; but I never gave up, and little by little, by using my strategies, he was learning the lesson that has made of him a man of respect.

If I continue to add so many of the cases in which I have seen how powerful words are, the book would be too long. I just added these examples to let the reader know that if we start molding the character of our kids from birth, by being firm and constant, but loving, understanding and fair, we are going to reap great satisfaction.

Our children, when they become adults, and see that they are out of trouble, would really appreciate us for taking our time to mold their character. However, is important to know that there may be factors out of our control, preventing us from succeeding in such a project; therefore, we need to observe them closely and analyze their behavior to make sure their incontrollable conduct is not a matter of a physical or psychological condition. If you have tried to control your child whose behavior is out of the norm, you need to find professional assistance.

Besides this, if by any means used, we do not get the results expected, we could feel satisfied, because we did our best. I personally thanks God for answering my prayer for wisdom to deal with my children. I praise him for guiding me in the development of those strategies I used, that really worked.

The intension behind the information presented in this chapter, is not of bragging, but of motivating the readers to never give up on such a project, which in the long run would bring them:

THE REWARD FOR BEING FIRM AND CONSTANT.

Chapter VIII
Practical Recomendatios

In an effort of raising my children to be responsible, honest, serious; but with a high self-esteem, I had to be very demanding and firm, yet, understanding and loving. The following are some of the practical recommendations which are based on the strategies I used to help my children in the process of becoming good citizens.

> **The first recommendation is as follows: Children need to be helped in the process of developing a high self-esteem, so they would not care of what others may think about them.**

It is sad to say, but there are many kids who have become victims of those called bullies to the point, that some of them have become suicidal. In my opinion, those bullies may be the result of child abuse or neglect, or of child over protection. While dealing with children for so many years, I noticed children, who somehow, were neglected by the person in charge of them, that they did not have the chance to develop their correct personality. This may be the reason they disturb those who are different than them.

But there is another side of the coin. There are other children who have been spoiled by the way they are treated. Some parents or care givers take sides when dealing with kids. This action may bring two different outcomes: the child that always gets the best treatment will feel superior to his siblings. On the other hand, the ones that do not get equal treatment, may get frustrated and rebellious.

And both sides would bring kids to become bullies.

Therefore, we need to help our children to really know who they are. This I always reminded my children. I also put emphasis on the idea of being proud of who they were, and to make sure to keep behaving with dignity, because time will come when we will reap what we sow. This advice took them to really ignored what others would think of them. But I also told them not to pay with the same coin.

The second advice is the following: We, adults, should help our children to respect the individual differences of other people.

Lack of respect towards people of other races, or ethnic groups, and lack of consideration towards people with some physical defect have created a crisis in schools, and in communities.

Sorry to say it this way, but many adults should be blamed for this. I have heard adults denigrating people from this or that country, and of this or that race or color, and finding faults on people, right in front of their children. Children have no notion of those differences.

As children, they play with any kid no matter who they are. But as they hear adults denigrating others, they may develop the same attitude. This brings to me the sad story of Dr. Martin Luther King Jr., who when he was in the elementary school, had a friend who was white. They really had fun together. But a sad afternoon, the white boy's mother saw them together, and she asked her son not to be with him anymore because he was black.

When Martin, (who at the time was only eight years old) received those shocking words, he felt so sad and disgusted, that when he became an adult, he decided to fight, in a peaceful way, against prejudice; which led him to become a martyr.

You could see in this story that Martin's friend had no idea of the color he had. His friend's mother was the one who put it in his mind. For kids to understand the races, or any other differences in people, it is good to let them observe nature. There is a lot of variety in nature. Trees, flowers, mountains, bodies of water, and so forth, are not the same, and the same thing could be seen in people. Not every person is physically the same; yet, we need each other in a direct or indirect way. I do not mean that everyone is going to be your close friend, but even if we are not interested on being friend with someone, we should show respect to him/her.

Even as a child, I do not know how I got the idea of not making fun of any kid in school, or in the neighbor-hood. Every time I heard a child making fun of another, I started to think that no one is to be blamed for being the way he/she was born. If we are white, black, skinny, fat or any other description, it is not our fault. We should make our children conscientious of this, so they would develop a sense of respect and consideration to others.

I made my kids aware that they should never find faults on anybody, neither make fun of them, because some day they were going to become parents, and their kids may come out to be whatever they criticized and I knew they would be very sad if others would make fun of them. Like the old saying, what goes around, comes around.

As third advice let me tell you that lying should not be allowed.

Speaking in general terms, children go through a stage of fantasy. They sometimes come up with some stories that are not true. They also tend to lie if they have done something out of what is expected, but does this mean we should not get them out of these fantasies? I personally believe we should. Otherwise they may become untrustworthy beings, which would be difficult to eradicate.

There is nothing so disgusting than an untruthful person. We need to find ways to stimulate our children to be honest. One way I encouraged my kids to tell the truth was by telling them that if they by any chance, would do something wrong, to tell me exactly how it happened, because sooner or later the truth would come out; and if they lie to me and later on I find out the truth, they were going to have double depravation: one for not telling the truth, and the other for the action.

However, this must be handled with wisdom. We need to be ready to give them a second chance, understanding that they are in the process of becoming adults, and they may sometimes make mistakes. Otherwise, next time they would be afraid to tell the truth. Just encourage them to be more careful next time, so this would not happen anymore.

The following incident was an experience I had with one of my sons who was five years old, and was already able to lie at such a short age. While I was working, his aunt was taking care of him. But for a while, he would tell his aunt: "Auntie, I don't want to eat here; I'll eat at home." But when I picked him up and got home, he would say: "Mommy, I already ate at auntie's house. I just want milk and cookies."

One evening his aunt called me and asked me if my son was having dinner at home. Then I realized he was fooling both of us. For a few days, we decided to pretend that we would never believe what he would say. Every time he told me something, I would say: "Are you coming up with another lie?"

This took him to express how he felt about the situation and said: "Oh God, why did I say that lie? Now they don't believe me at all!" Then I said to him: "This is the reason it is always good to tell the truth; otherwise, people would not show confidence in us and this would create a time of disgust."

An example of how one of my children showed how well he learned the lesson was the following: Some time ago, one of my sons and his family, came to Florida and we decided to take a trip to Disney World. And when we got ready to buy the tickets, a guy approached my son with a wonderful offer. If he would listen to some promotional meeting, he would be able to receive a ticket for free.

Doesn't it sound good? Well he accepted; but he was supposed to say he made more money than what he really made. The guy told him it didn't matter because they wouldn't do any investigation. So he accepted it. But then I started to notice that he wasn't at ease; he looked uncomfortable.

Then I asked him what's the matter, and this was his answer: "Mommy, those principles you instilled in me wouldn't allow me to take advantage of this. I really don't feel comfortable by just thinking about it." This experience confirmed me that I didn't waste my time.

Nevertheless, there may be someone who consider him stupid or silly for not taking advantage of the offer, but there isn't a greatest satisfaction than to feel good about oneself. He who walks in truth is free. A person who lies to get away with certain benefits becomes a slave of that lie thinking that sooner or later they may be caught in the lie. So, make sure that your children understand this.

> ***As the fourth advice I suggest to be very concern that the lack of respect is not tolerated in the house.***

I recommend being very careful in dealing with this issue. It's good to know that every person has the same rights. Many adults don't show equal respect to children, that at the same time are going to be disrespectful to others. For this reason, since children are very little, we have to help them develop respect to others, making sure of being a good example.

I was aware on how my children treated one another, and how they treated their friends, who were their playmates. It's well known that children from their early years tend to have dominion of the environment, trying by all means to be the center of attention. But to me there was no difference.

Yet, there were moments in which a little struggle took place, but it didn't last long, because I was there, ready to make them reason. Something I always did was to remind my kids to follow the golden rule: "Don't do to others what you don't want others to do to you." (a paraphrasis of Jesus' text) If we, human beings, would put this rule into practice, there wouldn't be so much disgrace in the world. This rule is key to mutual respect and consideration.

> ***My fifth advice is as follows. Avoid scolding or whipping your kids in front of strangers.***

When kids become preteenagers, they start to feel embarrassed if they are scolded or punished in front of strangers. But according to the words I'm about to express; I may be accused of not submitting to this rule. Well, my point is this: If the children become too disrespectful in front of strangers, they need to know that if they violate our rights in front of strangers, their rights will also be violated.

But if the situation is something that isn't related to that, take them to a private place, and call their attention in a way they'd appreciate; and this way they'll understand they are respected and appreciated.

As a sixth point my advice is to not allow your children to bring things to the house, if they don't have a real explanation of how they got it.

If I noticed that my kids brought something home that I didn't recognize, I would inquire how they got it. If we are not conscious that any wrong doing, no matter how insignificant it may be, can create a habit that later may get them into trouble, because thieves do not start stealing big things; they begin by stealing little things.

I started to use this method since my kids were toddlers. When my oldest son was only eighteen months, the backdoor neighbor, who really liked him, sometimes took him to her house. One afternoon, when he was coming back home, I noticed he was bringing a small ball, so I asked him: "Whose ball is that? And he answered with the little vocabulary he had: "A Shala." (De Sara) He meant to say it was Sara's ball. Then I asked him to turn back and give it back to her.

When Sara heard me, she said to never mind it, because it was just an insignificant thing. Then I explained to her that the ball may not have any value, but the lesson I was teaching my son, yes, had a lot of value. And made him return to ball.

Letting children to have their way because they are just little kids, has created a very sad situation in many families. Moral values must be enforced in children from the crib. The case about the ball is an example of how I dealt with this matter.

By the way, let me show you another case that proves how well my kids internalized my method. My youngest son, when his aunt gave him something, he would ask her to call me and report me that what he brings home was her gift. She always did. This is how I treated this aspect of discipline and my kids have proven me that my method really worked. They even respected each other things as they were growing up.

It's crucial to let our children know that what they bring home, whatever it is, they must show proof of ownership.

My seventh advice is something some readers may feel it's out of proportion, because it has to do with seriousness in doing business.

You may think I'm crazy for giving this advice if kids at an early age are not in business. But let me tell you that sometimes they do business with their playmates. To me, there's nothing more disgusting than a person that doesn't keep his/her word. That's why I made sure my kids were honest.

Nevertheless, one of my boys came to me and told me that he had sold his bike to one of his classmates for $30.00, but since he didn't have all the money, he promised him he will keep it until he had all the money. I didn't agree with the price since the bike had cost $130.00 and it was almost new; but since that was his decision, I agreed.

What a surprised he gave me! The next day he came home with $30.00; and when I asked him if the boy had the money already, he said: "I didn't sell it to him; I sold it to another student that had the money."

Someone probably would have said: "Woe, what a smart kid! He really knows how to do business!" But my reaction was of disgust. I asked him to get in the car and took him to the other boy's house to offer him an apology. You have no idea of how hard was for me to deal with this situation, because to face someone that we have failed, is not easy. But finally, he got in the car we got to the boy's house.

When the boy's father saw us there and heard me asking my son to get out of the car, he realized what was going on, and told me: "Don't worry; it's okay!" And I answered him this way: "What's important to me is not the way you feel about the situation, but the lesson I'm trying to teach my son, so in the future he would be a man of honor." Trying to be smart by being dishonest is the wrong means.

> ***Another important suggestion has to do with preventing our children from developing jealousy among them.***

What does the word jealousy mean? According to the WEBSTER NEW WORLD DICTIONARY it means suspicious of rivalry. In other words, it's fear of been defeated by another person in relation to affection and special favors.

This could bring parents to the extreme in order to prevent jealousy among their children, but this could also be counterproductive. If every time we buy a present to one of our kids because is his/her birthday, or any other special reason, or because they need it at the time; and to prevent the other kids from becoming jealous, we buy them something, we may be creating conflict, because let's say we're going through a financial situation, and can't afford to do this, they, as well as we are going to feel bad.

Thinking this way, since my children were little, I let them know the reason I was buying something for one of them. They got so used to this that I never noticed jealousy among them. Since this was part of their training, I didn't have any problem.

Nevertheless, we have to show them that when their time comes, they're going to be treated the same way. If they see equality in their treatment, they won't ever show signs of jealousy.

> ***Now let me present you advice number nine, which has to do with enforcing respect to other people's property starting at home.***

How would you feel if someone else takes your belongings just because he/she wants to? This was the strategy I used to train my children to respect one another belongings, and they learned the lesson so well, that they wouldn't take anything from the other, without permission.

This was learned so well, that even if they were facing a temptation, they wouldn't follow it. At one time, one of my sons was visiting a neighbor. She served him some food, he ate, took the dish to the sink and left. When she came to the dining room, she saw a $10.00 bill her husband had left on the table without her noticing it was there. She was so surprised that couldn't keep quiet. She called me and praise me for the child I had. Then I let her know that my children have clear in mind that what doesn't belong to them, has to be respected.

It's sad to say, but there are children that steal from their own parents. That is the reason we have to start guiding our kids through the right path at an early age. You may remember the incident I presented in a previous chapter, of my little one who used to take money from his daddy's drawer to buy icy at the candy store near our house, and how I dealt with the situation, that taught him not to take anything from anybody, including the family members. If I would've ignored his act, who knows what would be of him.

And the last recommendation is the following: It's very important to develop in children the capacity of self-evaluation by means of the moral values we've taught them.

This would help them to get to know themselves, and they'll be able to deal with the individual differences of those citizens that would be around, be it at school, playground and work. It's well known that we are surrounded by different beings, with different values and life purpose; and this produces a sense of competition, specially at schools. But if our kids have learned to develop a self-worth and self-respect, and over all loving care, they would be able to deal with any negative thing that may try to disturb them.

The suggestions I exposed in this chapter are a summary of the strategies I used to deal with my own children, and to handle all those children that were in my hands for those thirty-three years I worked as a teacher of every grade. I hope they serve as a resource for such an important project: OUR CHILDREN EDUCATION

Conclusion

One of Solomon's proverbs says: "The rod of correction gives wisdom, but a child left without it, brings shame to his mother. (Proverb 29:15) This text suggests the use of a rod, which stands for a stick for punishment. But we not necessarily have to go to that extreme, because of the Law of Child Abuse. This has become a controversial issue; not just recently, but for many years.

I still remember some of my students' mothers approaching me with the sad situation that they have lost control of their children (who already were teenagers) because they threat them with the law, and they were afraid to have to face a shameful situation with the law.

And my question is: "How could we prevent our children from putting us to shame?" By helping them to develop wisdom. But for that to happen, we, adults, need to set an example.

We need to use wisdom, patience and self-control; virtues that are necessary to handle discipline. And this would help them in the process of getting to know and appreciate themselves, which is necessary for the development of a mature character.

If they are proud of themselves, they would respect themselves, and this would help them to avoid whatever comes their way, that may cause them harm. This would help them to feel relaxed, and we would live at ease knowing that they are okay.

This work has been the product of many years of experience while dealing with so many children of different ages, plus the observation I have made of so many kids that have gotten out of control, even at an early age, which is taking many parents to worry about their future. This is the reason I took my time to share with the reader, how I dealt with the mission of helping children to become good citizens.

Priscila Gotay

I hope that the information exposed in this book would be a great resource to those who are looking for assistance in such a magnificent project which has been put in our hands: THE PROJECT OF MOLDING LIVES.

Epilogue

During my career as a teacher, I, as every teacher, sometimes suffered some disappointments, but now I could proudly express that they were not strong enough to prevent me from enjoying the satisfaction of seeing that my effort, not only to encourage them to learn the daily lesson, but also to learn life principles that would help them become citizens of good character.

There was nothing more satisfying to me than to see those students considered problematic, improve their attitude, by the way I approached them with respect and understanding. Often times is believed that children would not pay attention to what adults intend to do to help them become well behaved, but my experience has been that most of my students took their time to let me know, either by word of mouth, or by a written note, how much they appreciated the way I treated them, and admired the way I dealt with their shortcomings. I wish I would be able to include all of them on this section, but I am limiting myself to present only two of them, which may sound shocking to the reader, as well as it was to me.

Since I was licensed to work all the school levels, the school superintendent called me and asked me if I was willing to accept a challenge. At the time, I was working at an elementary school. I accepted the challenge and showed up there. When I was introduced to the teacher, she said that she refuses to work her last working year with those demons.

This was shocking to me; yet, I put myself on her shoes; I felt very sad but concerned. This made me think that after twenty-nine years working with children and teenagers, she should be tired and frustrated, which may be the reason the was feeling this way. My shock turned into compassion.

Well, I accepted the challenge, and this was going to be my first experience working in high school. But do not think the teacher was lying; she was right. Those students, specially the homeroom students, were acting like the description she made of them. Oh dear, most of them were disrespectful, irresponsible, distracted and outspoken. But thanks to the wisdom, self-control and loving care God has given me, I was able to deal with the situation with great satisfaction.

May 1983 to 1984 was the school year I started to work at this high school. On Teacher's Day of that school year, my homeroom students decided to give me a surprise. They have planned this, behind my back, and the school principal showed up in my classroom and told me not to go to the lunchroom, but to another teacher's classroom. So, I did. Even now, while writing about this incident, tears come to my eyes. They had for me a nice lunch and a present, but what really impressed me was a letter written by a student on behave of all of them. They gave her some words they wanted to express to me.

After so many years I still have this letter with me, in which there is an expression that really makes me happy when I read it, that reads as follows: … you saw that we were "falling down" (literal translation of the way some Puerto Ricans express which means, going on the wrong direction) and helped us to stand up. As I opened the letter that special day and read it, I considered it the greatest award of all.

On the next page, I'm including a copy of the letter which was written in Spanish, and a translation of it to English.

TRASLATION OF THE LETTER

May 8, 1984

To Mrs. Gotay,

    Mrs. Gotay, we want to thank you for being more than a teacher; you've been like a mother. Thank you for giving us an example of a good person. Thank you for understanding us the way you've done it to this day, because you have been there for us whenever we encountered some difficulties.

    And even if we've made some mistakes, you've helped us change our attitude by the way you talked to us. You saw that we were falling down, and helped us get on our feet, so we could go ahead in life as good citizens.

    Mrs. Gotay, we would depart from your class at the end of this month, but we would always have you in our mind, proud of having you as a teacher.

    Thank you once again. We all love you and won't ever forget you.

Sincerely,
Your 1st. period class 10-3

5/13/94

A la Sra.: Pricila Gotay.

Gotay te damos gracias como maestra, por portarte con nosotros como si fuera nuestra mamá. Gracias por saber darnos un buen ejemplo como persona, gracias por comprendernos como nos has comprendido hasta ahora, porque en los momentos más difíciles tú nos has ayudado, nos has visto caer y nos has ayudado a levantarnos, nos has dado ánimos para seguir adelante en la vida, y para ser buenos ciudadanos. Gotay nos apartamos de tu lado a fines de este mes, pero siempre te tendremos en nuestras mentes y te recordaremos con aquello (como amiga nos has aconsejado, nos has ayudado y te estamos agradecidos por todo.

Gracias una vez más, te queremos mucho y no te olvidaremos.

Att.

The next is the copy of a letter a group of students at More Haven Jr. Sr. High school in Florida, where I had the opportunity to teach Spanish. This was my first and only experience as a Spanish teacher, which I consider a marvelous experience.

At the end this school year I have decided to return to my country, Puerto Rico. And the last school day, my students handed me the following letter which I have decided to include as prove of the way I have dealt with children.

Date: June 1st. 1989

Priscila Gotay

Buena Suerte   6-1-89

To: Mrs. Gotay;
 Well, it's time for us to say Good Bye. We have to leave you because you're such a sweet teacher. I hope that you will not forget your 7th period class: Ronald Thompson, Eleanor Scott, Juanita Garcia, Mylene Smith, Belinda Graham, Cherish Fries, Michelle Pullen, Wren Espinoza, Patricia Madrigal, Brad Parker, Vincent Hyatt, Anthony Taylor, Tracie McPherson, Shon Roberts, Patti Elzey. Even though we were bad at times, we still appreciate everything you tried to do for us. Believe it or not our class learned a lot of Spanish.
 When you go back to Puerto Rico tell your students that the kids over here are great. So, don't forget we are going to miss you dearly. We really do hate to see you leave because you're the best Spanish teacher Moore Haven Jr. Sr. High School ever had. You're such an open and kind hearted person. You don't only act like a school teacher you also act as a friend. That's one of the good qualities you have so don't ever lose that special quality.
 Nice having you as a teacher. Good luck in Puerto Rico.

www.ingramcontent.com/pod-product-compliance
Ingram Content Group UK Ltd.
Pitfield, Milton Keynes, MK11 3LW, UK
UKHW022221230426
12048UKWH00016BA/993